What's Right About Wrong Answers

look like this.

Why do you think so?

parallelograms are slanted.

P   R

Learning from Math Mistakes, Grades 4–5

Stenhouse Publishers
Portland, Maine

Nancy C. Anderson

Stenhouse Publishers
www.stenhouse.com

Library of Congress Cataloging-in-Publication Data
Names: Anderson, Nancy, 1975–
Title: What's right about wrong answers : learning from math mistakes,
     grades 4–5 / Nancy Anderson.
Description: Portland, Maine : Stenhouse Publishers, [2016] | Includes
     bibliographical references and index.
Identifiers: LCCN 2016034132 (print) | LCCN 2016038324 (ebook) | ISBN
     9781625310866 (pbk. : alk. paper) | ISBN 9781625310873 (ebook)
Subjects: LCSH: Mathematics—Study and teaching (Elementary) |
     Problem solving. | Iterative methods (Mathematics) | Errors.
Classification: LCC QA135.6 .A525 2016 (print) | LCC QA135.6 (ebook)
     | DDC 372.7/049—dc23
LC record available at https://lccn.loc.gov/2016034132

Cover design, interior design, and typesetting by Martha Drury
Illustrations by Ellie Gill

Manufactured in the United States of America

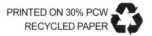
PRINTED ON 30% PCW
RECYCLED PAPER

23 22 21 20 19 18 17   9 8 7 6 5 4 3 2 1

Contents

Acknowledgments

Although my name is the only one to appear on the front cover, this book reflects the efforts of an entire group of people. I would like to thank Toby Gordon and the entire production team at Stenhouse for believing in this project and guiding its development through every phase. I am so very grateful to my family for giving me the time and space to write. Thank you to my colleagues for the wonderful discussions we have shared about the value of students' mistakes. And, most of all, thank you to all of the students I've had the honor of teaching over the past twenty years. I especially wish to thank those students who "err and come short again and again" and still persist until their hard work pays off. Your tenacity and courage motivate me as a math learner and inspire me to be a better teacher. Thank you.

Introduction

My interest in the relationship between mistakes and learning began when I was a student studying calculus. Like all math students, I worked hard to understand the course material. When I was confused about particular problems or made mistakes on test or homework items, I asked my professors for help and listened intently as they explained the correct solution strategies. But even when these explanations were clear and concise and even when I could follow them step-by-step, I was often still confused. Although I understood the steps and logic in their work, when I looked down at my own, I still didn't see what made my answer wrong. Making sense of a sound approach did not teach me what was wrong with my approach. And having my mistakes unresolved left me feeling unsure whether I really understood the concepts or whether I'd be able to avoid similar mistakes in the future.

The frustration I felt about my unresolved mistakes took on greater meaning when I read the National Research Council's *How People Learn* (Bransford, Brown, and Cocking 2000). In this book I learned that correct ideas do not necessarily replace misconceptions during the learning process. Instead, new ideas are connected to prior conceptions—including faulty ones. As an example, the authors describe what often happens when a young child is told that the Earth is round instead of flat. When children first encounter this idea, they add the idea of roundness to their image of a flat world. Instead of a ball, children envision the Earth as a pancake—round and flat. When I read this example, I suddenly realized exactly why I'd been so frustrated by my professors' careful and correct explanations. I didn't need explanations that focused on correct solution strategies but help in finding the flaw in my approach. So, instead of asking my professors to show me how to solve a problem correctly, I asked them to look at my work and help me figure out what I did wrong and why it was wrong. The effect on my learning was profound. I was able to identify and unravel my misconceptions and use my mistakes to find correct solution strategies.

My classroom instruction reflects what I learned as a student about the role of mistakes in developing understanding. First, I never use the phrase *careless error* to describe my students' mistakes. Mistakes do not show a lack of care but rather show evidence that students are trying to make sense of a problem by connecting it to what they already know. Second, I plan my lessons so that they focus on mistakes. I anticipate likely mistakes and think about how I will respond when I see these errors during class. Finally, I spend as much time in class talking about mistakes as I do talking about correct answers. In addition to sharing sound approaches, we talk as a class about flawed strategies. We discuss why a particular error might occur, why it is wrong, and how we can use the mistake to find the correct approach. These discussions have not only helped my students learn more math but also helped them realize the essential role of mistakes in their learning.

I wrote this book as a support to classroom teachers who are also interested in using error analysis as a classroom activity for students. The problems and mistakes featured in the book are based on my experiences in the classroom as a teacher and math coach as well as related research from the field of elementary mathematics education. I hope the student activities and support materials for teachers help classroom communities embrace mistakes as invaluable tools to help students understand math deeply.

Why Talk About Mistakes in Math Class?

When we make mistakes, our brains spark and grow.

—Jo Boaler

If students are learning, they are making mistakes. Very few of these mistakes are the result of carelessness, random guessing, or a lack of effort. Instead, students' mistakes often contain sound ideas and relevant prior knowledge and signal that they are trying to figure out what makes sense. Although they vary in scope and complexity, students' mistakes in math typically fall into one of the following categories:

- Overgeneralizing about a computational procedure or problem-solving strategy
- Using a strategy based on a faulty premise (i.e., a misconception)
- Applying a procedure or formula that does not fit the particulars of a problem
- Attending to surface or superficial characteristics of a task
- Using a flawed definition of a mathematical term
- Forming a faulty connection between two or more ideas

Some teachers believe that talking about mistakes in math class will impede student learning. Teachers fear that the discussion will draw students' attention to the errors, causing them to become ingrained in their mathematical tool kits. Or teachers worry that talking about errors will encourage students to be careless or sloppy with their work. Although these are reasonable beliefs, they are not supported by research on the efficacy of error analysis as an instructional tool for students. Specifically, talking about mistakes does not cause students to make more mistakes nor does it encourage them to be careless about their work. Instead, talking about students' mistakes and why they are wrong helps students understand math deeply. Four particular ideas about the relationship between mistakes and learning are highlighted here.

- **It is not possible to learn without making mistakes.** Being wrong is a sign that someone is trying to understand, to make connections, and to figure out what makes sense. Being wrong in math is similar to making mistakes in other domains. You can't learn to hit a three-point shot without missing a lot of shots. You can't learn to play a piece of music correctly without striking a lot of wrong notes. In math, you can't identify the correct pathways without first encountering the faulty ones. Therefore, if teachers want to give students an accurate portrayal of what it means to learn math, we must acknowledge errors as a required part of the learning process. When we spend class time talking about mistakes, we let students know that trying out ideas, getting things wrong, and revising one's thinking are the ways that learners develop deep understanding.

- **Attending to mistakes is associated with a growth mind-set.** Thanks to the research of Carol Dweck (2006) and Jo Boaler (2009, 2016), we know now that students' beliefs about their learning affect how well they learn. Specifically, students with a growth mind-set—an attitude that focuses on learning and improvement (instead of ability)—attend very closely to their errors as they work toward a solution (Boaler 2016; Moser et al. 2011). For these students, solving the problem *and* checking their work are the same, not separate, processes. These students seem to have an awareness that making mistakes is a part of learning, and they tend to use their errors as problem-solving tools. This relationship suggests that classroom teachers may be able to help students develop a growth mind-set by promoting mistakes as a source of learning.

- **Talking about mistakes helps students eliminate faulty misconceptions.** It's a common belief that we help students learn by talking about correct solution strategies and sound ideas. But focusing learners' attention on what *is* correct does not eliminate misconceptions. If misconceptions are not addressed directly, students build new ideas on top of prior misconceptions (Bransford, Brown, and Cocking 2000). Talking about mistakes in math class puts a spotlight on faulty ideas so that they can be addressed and dismantled.

- **Mistakes that are solutions in progress can lead to correct solution strategies.** Posting a flawed solution strategy to a problem and talking about why the strategy is flawed illuminates the concepts that are required to formulate a correct approach. When students talk about their mistakes and why they are flawed, mistakes become *solutions in progress* rather than missteps to be avoided (Tugend 2011). Students can learn to view their mistakes as clues that lead to sound approaches. When a mistake occurs in the midst of a solution strategy, students should not think, "I have to start all over." Instead, if they can reflect on the mistake and why it is wrong, they can use it to help them move toward the correct solution.

What Kinds of Student Activities Are Included Here?

This book provides error analysis tasks for students. The activities focus on important ideas in grades four and five mathematics and the mistakes that typically occur as students develop understanding of these big ideas. The activities feature the mistakes of fictionalized students and are presented using three different formats.

Comic Strips: These activities feature comic strip depictions of elementary students talking about a mathematical problem, computation, or concept. At one point in the comic strip, a student makes a mistake. Students read the comic strip and then answer a set of questions that focus on addressing and resolving the error.

***Dear Professor Math* Writing Prompts:** These activities feature letters to Professor Math, a fictitious math expert who offers advice to confused students. Each letter focuses on an unresolved error, misconception, or question about a particular skill or idea. Students read the letter, talk about the highlighted mistake or misconception, and write a response to the confused student from the perspective of Professor Math.

Sample Student Work: These activities show a written solution to a math problem or computation. Each piece of student work contains at least one mistake. Students examine the written work, identify the errors and their roots, and offer ideas for correction.

How Are the Activities Formatted?

Each of the twenty-two student activities is accompanied by a set of teaching notes that include the following information.

Overview	Summarizes the mathematical content, highlighted mistake, and the structure of the activity.
Common Core Connections	Lists the Common Core content standards with which the activity is aligned.
Before You Use This Activity	Specifies the prerequisite knowledge or prior experiences that students need in order to complete the activity.
Materials	Lists all required reproducibles, math manipulatives, or other tools needed to complete the activity.
Digging Deeper into the Math	Unpacks the big ideas of the activity by describing the relevant mathematics, addressing the possible roots of the featured mistake, and explaining why the error should be addressed in class.
Teaching Notes	Provides suggestions on how to implement the activity by describing teaching strategies, discussion questions, and talk moves that will keep the targeted mistake and corresponding mathematical ideas at the focus of the instruction.
Extending the Activity	Provides two or three additional classroom tasks that teachers can use to deepen students' thinking or assess their understanding.

How to Use This Book

Each of the twenty-two student activities can be used to enhance units of instruction. It is recommended that teachers embed an activity within the unit of study that most closely relates to the mathematics in the activity. For example, the activity on area of rectangles, *Measuring Area: Clarifying Ideas About Units*, would fit nicely within a unit on two-dimensional measurement. It's also highly recommended that teachers use each activity after students already have basic understandings about the content and after they have begun to generate strategies for a particular skill. Teachers may even want to wait until they see and hear some of the misconceptions featured in a particular task before using the task in class. This approach will help students see the relevance of a task and connect the big ideas to their own mistakes and learning. Finally, this book is intended to supplement teachers' own work with error analysis. Teachers should continue to use mistakes derived from their own students' work as instructional tools in math class. A key aim of this book is to help teachers and students create a classroom climate where talking about mistakes—the ones featured in this book and the ones that occur organically in class—is a regular and productive instructional routine.

How Does This Resource Align with the Common Core?

This resource supports the Common Core in three key ways:

- Each student activity is closely aligned with specific grade-level Standards for Mathematical Content. These standards are identified in the lesson plan for each activity in a section entitled, "Teaching with the Common Core."
- Four specific Standards for Mathematical Practice are prominent throughout the entire book.
  - *Practice 1: Make sense of problems and persevere in solving them.* This resource encourages students to use mistakes as pathways toward correct solution strategies so that they become persistent problem solvers.
  - *Practice 3: Construct viable arguments and critique the reasoning of others.* The mistakes featured in this book are derived from common mistakes from actual students. By talking about the sources and resolutions of these mistakes, students gain valuable experience assessing and evaluating the work of fellow student mathematicians.
  - *Practice 5: Use appropriate tools strategically.* Many of the mistakes in the book feature the work of students who are struggling to use common elementary math tools, such as number lines and area models. Discussing these mistakes can draw students' attention toward the most salient aspects of these tools so that they learn how to use them appropriately.
  - *Practice 6: Attend to precision.* The activities in the book emphasize the confusion that can arise as the result of miscalculations, misuse of symbols, and imprecise definitions. This awareness can motivate students to express themselves with greater precision when striving to develop deep understanding of key mathematical ideas.
- The format of the activities helps students prepare for assessments aligned with the Common Core. These assessments typically include items that focus on analyzing mathematical mistakes. Completing the activities in this book provides students with engaging ways to prepare for these assessment items.

Chapter 1

Whole–Number Multiplication and Division

Whole-number multiplication and division are focal points of students' work with number and operations in grades four and five. Instructional goals include understanding the different interpretations of these operations, solving multistep problems, computing with multidigit numbers, and interpreting the results of those computations (e.g., remainders). The seven activities in this chapter focus on common mistakes and misconceptions related to these instructional goals. The activities help students develop a robust understanding of multiplication and division by encouraging them to connect computational procedures to underlying skills and apply sound strategies to problem scenarios.

Activity 1.1   Comparing Multiplication Models: Thinking Deeply About Arrays

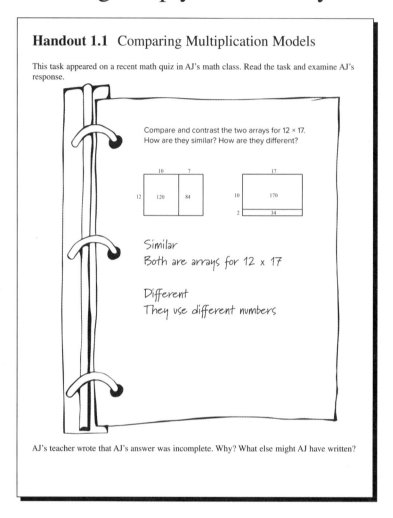

Handout 1.1 Comparing Multiplication Models

This task appeared on a recent math quiz in AJ's math class. Read the task and examine AJ's response.

Compare and contrast the two arrays for 12 × 17. How are they similar? How are they different?

Similar
Both are arrays for 12 x 17

Different
They use different numbers

AJ's teacher wrote that AJ's answer was incomplete. Why? What else might AJ have written?

Overview

This activity features the work of a student who is having difficulty using the big ideas of multiplication to explain how two arrays are similar and different. Discussing the sample student work gives students the opportunity to think deeply about the meaning of each factor in a multiplication computation and helps students develop proficiency using multiples of ten to compute larger products.

Common Core Connections

Number and Operations in Base Ten, 4.B.5

Before You Use This Activity

Before you use this activity in class, be sure students have had prior experiences using open or unmarked arrays to represent multiplication combinations and products of two-digit numbers. See "Digging Deeper into the Math" for more information about arrays and multiplication.

Materials (in Appendix) Handout 1.1, *Comparing Multiplication Models*

Digging Deeper into the Math   Arrays are a very effective model for helping students explore multiplication. An array is created by arranging squares into rows and columns. Because multiplication is interpreted as putting equal groups together, each row contains the same number of squares as all of the other rows. Figure 1.1 shows the product of 4 × 6.

Figure 1.1

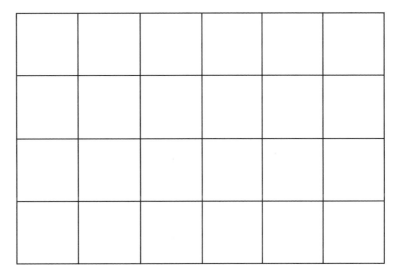

After students work with arrays that show each individual square in each row and column, they can create open (or unmarked, empty, or blank) arrays. These arrays do not show the individual squares in each row or column and are not drawn to scale. Instead, the dimensions of the arrays as well as the idea of multiplication as putting equal groups together are used to determine areas and to compute products. An open array for 4 × 6 is pictured in Figure 1.2.

Figure 1.2

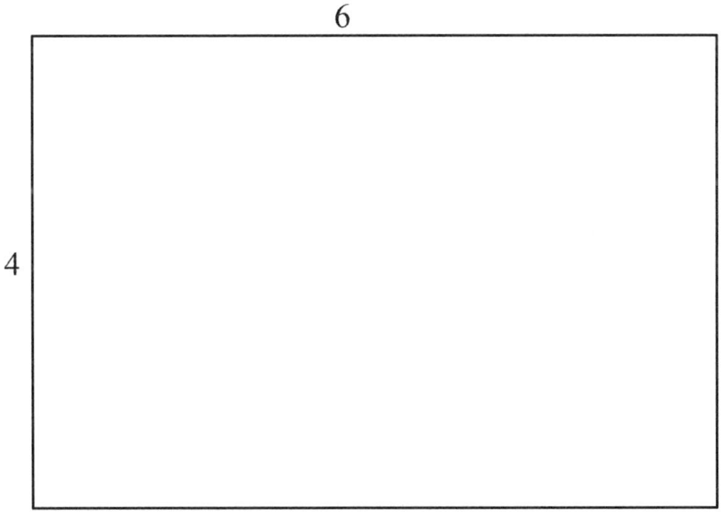

6

4

Open arrays are particularly helpful for computing products of two-digit numbers. Students can split the larger array into smaller pieces, or chunks, and use known number combinations to figure out the calculations. When students use open arrays to compute products, they are working with a visual representation of the distributive property. Two different arrays for the computation 12 × 17 are pictured in Figure 1.3.

Figure 1.3

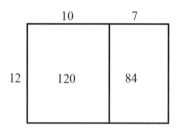

$12 \times 17 = (12 \times 10) + (12 \times 7) = 204$ $12 \times 17 = (10 \times 17) + (2 \times 17) = 204$

When students use open arrays to find products, they need to make choices about how to partition the larger array. Some students may partition the array by breaking up the total number of groups. Or they may partition the size of each group. Students may even do both. Multiples of ten (often known as *friendly numbers*) can be very helpful when partitioning arrays. Both examples use multiples of ten to compute 12 × 17 using smaller, friendlier parts.

Making efficient choices about how to partition open arrays to compute products is not an easy task. As students choose how to partition the array, they must conserve the original values of the two factors. When an array is partitioned into smaller pieces, the parts (i.e., the sizes of the rows and columns) must add up to the values of the two original factors. (*Note*: Some readers may notice that it is possible to change the value of one factor as long as the solver then compensates for this change later on in the procedure. An example of this strategy is given in the activity extensions.) Comparing two different open arrays for the same computation is an effective way to help students focus on this idea. Talking about what two arrays have in common for a particular computation can help students think about conservation as well as the role of friendly numbers in partitioning arrays.

Teaching Notes

1. Begin this task by posting the arrays and writing prompt embedded in the sample student work. Ask students to write their own response describing how the two arrays are similar and different.
2. Pass out Handout 1.1, *Comparing Multiplication Models*. Ask students to review and edit the sample work on their own before sharing their ideas with a partner. Use this time to identify speakers for the whole-class discussion. (See Step 3 for suggestions on what to listen for.)
3. Call the class together for a whole-class discussion.

    a.   Focus the discussion on what is missing from the student's response. You might say, "The student wrote one similarity and one difference. Why do you think the teacher marked the answer 'incomplete'?" Students should notice that the student's response is unspecific. The similarity really doesn't describe anything about the arrays. The difference is an accurate observation, but it doesn't explain why the numbers are different or connect these numbers to the arrays.

    b.   Talk about how to improve the explanation. Students' comments may include the following:

        a.   Both arrays interpret 12 × 17 as 12 rows of 17.

        b.   Both arrays show "friendly" or smaller arrays within the bigger array.

        c.   The arrays differ in how they are divided.

        d.   The first array is separated into rows of 10 plus 7; it shows the product using 12 rows of 10 plus 12 rows of 7.

        e.   The second array is separated into 10 rows plus 2 rows; it shows the array as 10 rows of 17 plus 2 more rows of 17.

        f.   Both arrays use the number 10 because it is easy to multiply a number by 10.

    c.   Ask students whether both arrays are accurate representations of the problem. Students should note that both representations maintain the value of each factor when it is split into smaller parts.

4.   Give students time to revisit their written answers so that they can incorporate the ideas from the class discussion.

Extending the Activity

1.   Copy the arrays shown in Figure 1.4 on the whiteboard. Pose the following problem to students:

Imagine a teacher asked a student how the two arrays were similar and how they were different. Imagine the student said, "They are similar because they are both arrays for 21 × 23. They are different because they use different numbers." Why might the teacher consider this answer "incomplete"? What else might the student write?

Figure 1.4

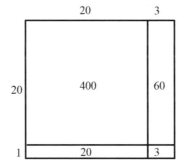
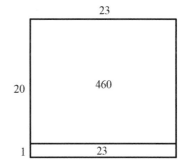

(Possible response: The answer needs more details. The student's answer does not focus on how the arrays have been partitioned. The student should explain that both arrays use friendly numbers to find the product of *21 × 23*. But one array partitions both the number of rows and size of the rows into parts. The second array only breaks the number of rows into two parts.)

2. Post the two arrays featured in the original problem for 12 × 17. Post the two equations below. Ask students to connect each number sentence to the array that it represents. Which number sentence more closely matches which array?

   a. $12 \times 17 = 12 \times (10 + 7) = (12 \times 10) + (12 \times 7) = 120 + 84 = 204$
   b. $12 \times 17 = (10 + 2) \times 17 = (10 \times 17) + (2 \times 17) = 170 + 34 = 204$

   (Possible response: The first number sentence matches the first array, which shows two rectangles with dimensions 12 × 10 and 12 × 7. The second number sentence matches the second array, which shows two rectangles with dimensions 10 × 17 and 2 × 17.)

3. Post the array in Figure 1.5 and pose the following problem to students:

   Imagine a student, ZZ, used the array and number sentence below to compute 19 × 41. His friend, TR, said, "That won't work. The problem is 19 × 41 but you used 20 × 41. Something is wrong." Do you agree with TR? Why or why not?

Figure 1.5

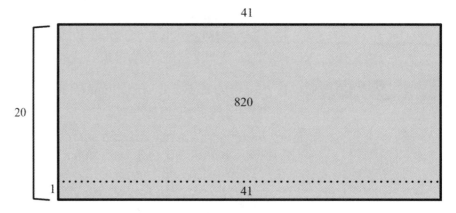

$$20 \times 41 - 41 = 820 - 41 = 779$$

(Possible response: Students should notice that ZZ's array offers an acceptable way to find the product. He is using the array for 20 × 41 to find the product of 19 × 41 by drawing 20 rows of 41 and then taking away one row of 41.)

Activity 1.2   Solving a Multiplication Word Problem: Rethinking Key Words

Handout 1.2 Solving a Multiplication Word Problem

Read the comic. Then answer the questions that follow.

Questions:
1.   Why did BB choose multiplication as a strategy for solving the problem?
2.   Is BB's strategy correct? Why or why not?

Overview

The comic strip featured in this activity focuses on the use of key words as a strategy for choosing the correct operation for a particular word problem. In the comic strip, a student chooses multiplication as the operation for solving a problem because the word *groups* appears in the problem. Talking about this mistake gives students the opportunity to discuss the limitations of key words and to generate more reliable strategies for choosing an appropriate operation.

Common Core Connections

Operations and Algebraic Thinking, 4.A.3

Before You Use This Activity

Before they explore this activity, students should have prior experiences thinking about multiplication in terms of equal groups.

Materials (in Appendix) Handout 1.2, *Solving a Multiplication Word Problem*

Digging Deeper into the Math

When students solve a word problem, they must think carefully about which operation (or operations) will yield the correct solution. Students often rely on a variety of strategies when they think about which operation to choose to solve a word problem. One common strategy is to look for specific, or *key*, words or phrases that are typically associated with one particular operation. For example, students may connect the word *groups* with multiplication and apply this operation—by default—when they find this word in the text of a problem. Although this strategy may seem reasonable, it is ultimately unreliable given that the word *groups* can be associated with other operations. For example, consider the following problem: *There are 24 cans of juice packaged in groups of 6. How many packages are there?* Even though this problem includes the word *groups*, multiplying 24 by 6 would not yield the correct solution. Instead of key words, students should choose the correct operation by focusing on the meaning of the numbers in the problem and the relationship between those numbers. In the previous example, division is the appropriate choice (i.e., $24 \div 6 = 4$) because we are given the total and the size of each group. Choosing an appropriate operation is particularly important when solving multistep word problems. Classroom instruction should aim to help students with this endeavor by making explicit connections between the actions and relationships in the problem and the related mathematical operations.

Teaching Notes

1. Begin the discussion by posting the word problem embedded in the comic. Ask students to solve the word problem on their own before sharing their strategies with a partner.

2. Pass out Handout 1.2, *Solving a Multiplication Word Problem*. Ask students to respond to the writing prompt on their own before talking with a partner.

3. Call the class together for a whole-class discussion.

   a. First, talk about why BB might think the solution requires multiplication. Students may respond that BB notices the word *groups* in the story problem and uses that to decide that the solution strategy requires multiplication.

   b. Talk about why BB's reasoning is incorrect. Students' ideas may include the following:

      i. If BB were correct, there would be $30 \times 3 = 90$ students raking leaves. But this cannot be correct because we are told that the total is 30 students.

      ii. If BB were correct, each of 90 groups filled 5 bags. But there are not 90 groups of students raking leaves.

   c. Share ideas for solving the problem correctly. Students may suggest using division to find the number of groups of students ($30 \div 3 = 10$)

and then multiplying $5 \times 10 = 50$ to find the total number of bags of leaves filled by all the students.

d. Talk about the merits and limitations of using key words, especially when solving multiplication and division problems. Because multiplication often involves groups of numbers, it makes sense to think that a problem with the word *groups* may require multiplication. But we also talk about groups when we divide. This is why we can't just automatically use multiplication when we see the word *groups*. (See, "Digging Deeper into the Math" for more information.) Instead, we need to focus on the actions described in the problem and the relationships between the numbers in the problem to decide which operation to use. This is especially important when students are solving multistep problems that involve more than one operation.

4. Give students time to revisit their written answers so that they can incorporate the ideas from the class discussion.

Extending the Activity

1. Pose the following story problem and the answer that follows to students:

Nancy bought 12 packs of pineapple juice. There are 4 cans in each pack. She drinks 2 cans of juice each week. She has enough cans for how many weeks?

One student's answer: $12 \times 4 \times 2 = 96$. How might a student reach this answer? Why is the answer wrong? How could the student fix the mistake?

(Possible response: A student could reach the given answer if she or he considers the word *packs* as a clue for using multiplication. This answer is not correct because we need to divide 48 cans into groups of 2 since Nancy drinks 2 cans per week. The correct answer is 24. Nancy has $12 \times 4 = 48$ cans in all. She drinks 2 of these cans each week. Since $48 \div 2 = 24$, Nancy has enough cans for 24 weeks.)

2. Pose the following problem to students:

Four friends shared a jumbo pack of erasers. Each friend got 20 erasers. How many erasers were in the package?

Ask students how they would respond if a friend said that he solved this problem using division ($20 \div 4 = 5$) because the problem has the word *shared* in it. What would they say in response to their friend's reasoning? (Possible response: Using the word *shared* as a clue for division is not a reliable strategy. The word *shared* could be used to describe any of the four operations, not just division. Even though this problem includes the word *shared*, we actually need to multiply to find the solution. Because we are told the number of groups and the number in each group, we can find the total number in the package by multiplying $4 \times 20 = 80$.)

Activity 1.3   Solving a Comparison Word Problem: What Does "Times as Much" Really Mean?

Handout 1.3   Solving a Comparison Word Problem

Read the comic. Then answer the questions that follow.

Questions:
1.   Why did JT use the equation $3 \times 10 + 10 = 40$ to solve the problem?
2.   Do you think the price of the sweatshirt is $30 or $40? Explain.

The comic strip featured in this activity focuses on a story problem that involves the *compare* interpretation of multiplication. In the comic strip, a student describes how she solved the problem by reasoning about the comparison factor as the difference between the two numbers. Discussing this mistake provides students with an opportunity to differentiate between additive and multiplicative comparison.

Operations and Algebraic Thinking, 4.A.1, 4.A.2

Before you use this activity in class, spend time talking about the meaning of phrases such as *three times as many*. It may be helpful to model these types of comparisons using concrete manipulatives. For example, consider the following problem:

> *EJ has 2 erasers. JR has 3 times as many erasers. How many erasers does JR have?*

Ask students to show their solutions using square tiles. Students may use 2 square tiles for EJ's erasers and 6 tiles for JR's erasers. Or, students may instead use 1 tile to represent 2 erasers and 3 tiles to represent 6 erasers. Be sure students can connect each of these models to the constraints of the problem and explain how the two models are similar. (See Figure 1.6.)

Figure 1.6

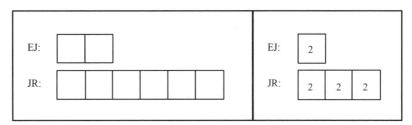

Materials (in Appendix)

Handout 1.3, *Solving a Comparison Word Problem*
square tiles (optional)

Digging Deeper into the Math

Multiplicative compare (or comparison) problems describe situations in which multiplication is used to compare two numbers. When we model these situations with a multiplicative expression, the first factor is the *comparison factor* and reveals the number of times the second factor must be repeated or copied. One common error that occurs when students work with multiplicative compare problems is thinking that the comparison factor refers to the difference between the numbers. For example, if asked to solve the problem featured in this activity (*A concert t-shirt costs $10. A concert sweatshirt costs 3 times as much. What is the price of the sweatshirt?*), students sometimes think that the *difference* between the two numbers is 30. This misconception is likely rooted in students' work with addition. When we think about comparison in terms of additive relationships, we do compute the difference between the two numbers. Students benefit from experiences and models that help them distinguish between additive comparison (i.e., differences) and multiplicative comparison. Bar diagrams (a.k.a. tape diagrams) provide an effective tool for helping students make this distinction. In these diagrams, one bar is used to represent the quantity or size of one group. The bar is then repeated the same number of times as the comparison factor. (See Figure 1.7.)

Figure 1.7

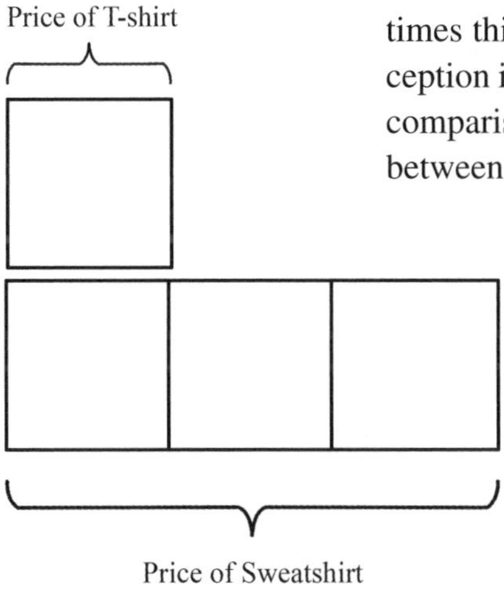

Price of T-shirt

Price of Sweatshirt

When using bar diagrams to model compare problems, it is important to connect the related multiplication equation (e.g., $10 \times 3 = 30$) to the diagram. Making connections between representations is an effective way to help students develop a deep understanding of this interpretation of multiplication.

1. Post the word problem embedded in the comic. Ask students to solve the word problem on their own before sharing their strategies and solutions with their partners.

2. Pass out the Handout 1.3, *Solving a Comparison Word Problem.* Ask students to respond to the writing prompt on their own before talking with a partner. Listen in on students' conversations and use that information to help you select speakers for the whole-class discussion.

3. Call the class together for a whole-class discussion.

   a. Do not reveal whether JT's strategy and solution are correct. Instead, ask students to choose a position—either for or against $40 as the cost for the sweatshirt—and explain their reasoning. Write their ideas on the board. Students' ideas may include the following:

JT's strategy is correct	**JT's strategy is incorrect**
• "3 times 10" is what we have to add to the price of the t-shirt to get the price of the sweatshirt • If the sweatshirt costs 3 times as much as the t-shirt, it must be $30 more than the t-shirt. • Because the t-shirt is $10, we need to add 30 + 10 to get the price of the sweatshirt.	• If you repeat the price of the t-shirt 3 times, you get the price of the sweatshirt. • The number 3 is telling us how many times to repeat 10 to get the price of the sweatshirt. • If we say the price is 3 times the other price, we are comparing the prices and *not* the difference between them. • We can use a bar diagram to show that the price of the sweatshirt is $30, or 3 times $10. Price of T-shirt Price of Sweatshirt

4. After approximately 10 minutes, ask students to reflect on the comments on the board silently on their own. Give students a chance to revise their original positions.

5. Ask students to share their ideas with a partner. Use this information to decide how to wrap up the discussion. For example, if the class remains split, you may want to table the discussion and continue to explore, model, and solve multiplicative comparison problems during the next several math classes. Or if the majority of students are convinced that JT's strategy is flawed and can explain why the answer is $3 \times 10 = 30$, wrap up by calling on a few students to explain their thinking.

6. Give students time to revisit their written answers so that they can incorporate the ideas from the class discussion.

Extending the Activity

1. Post this story problem and the student solution that follows:

   A small bag of pretzels contains 12 pretzels. The large bag contains 4 times as many pretzels. How many pretzels does the large bag contain?

   One student's solution:
   $4 \times 12 = 48$ (So the large bag must have 48 more pretzels than the small bag.)
   $48 + 12 = 60$
   Answer: There are 60 pretzels in the large bag.

   Ask students to explain whether they think the student's solution is correct or incorrect.
   (Possible response: The solution is incorrect. Because the large bag contains 4 times as many pretzels, we should repeat the number of pretzels in the small bag, 12, a total of 4 times to find the number in the large bag: $4 \times 12 = 48$.)

2. Post the story problem and the student solution that follows.

   Thirty-two students participate in an after-school recycling club. The hiking club has 4 times fewer participants. How many students are in the hiking club?

   One student's solution:
   $32 \div 4 = 8$ (So there are 8 fewer students in the hiking club.)
   $32 - 8 = 24$
   Answer: There are 24 students in the hiking club.

   Is the solution correct or incorrect?

   (Possible response: The solution is incorrect. Because the hiking club has four times fewer students, we need to find what number repeated four times is 32. The number of students in the hiking club is 8 because $4 \times 8 = 32$.)

Activity 1.4   Division with Remainders: Making Sense of What's Left Over

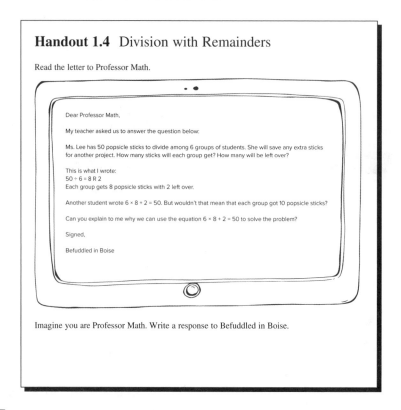

Handout 1.4 Division with Remainders

Read the letter to Professor Math.

Dear Professor Math,

My teacher asked us to answer the question below:

Ms. Lee has 50 popsicle sticks to divide among 6 groups of students. She will save any extra sticks for another project. How many sticks will each group get? How many will be left over?

This is what I wrote:
50 ÷ 6 = 8 R 2
Each group gets 8 popsicle sticks with 2 left over.

Another student wrote 6 × 8 + 2 = 50. But wouldn't that mean that each group got 10 popsicle sticks?

Can you explain to me why we can use the equation 6 × 8 + 2 = 50 to solve the problem?

Signed,

Befuddled in Boise

Imagine you are Professor Math. Write a response to Befuddled in Boise.

Overview

This activity focuses on division with remainders. The *Dear Professor Math* letters feature two different ways to represent the remainder when 50 is divided by 6. Discussing the two representations gives students the opportunity to think deeply about the meaning of the remainder in a division computation and the different ways it can be represented with symbols.

Common Core Connections

Number and Operations in Base Ten, 4.B.6

Before You Use This Activity

Before you use this activity, students should have had prior experiences working with remainders and interpreting common symbols associated with division with remainders (e.g., 50 ÷ 6 = 8 R 2.)

Materials (in Appendix)

Handout 1.4, *Division with Remainders*

Digging Deeper into the Math

Solving division problems in which the divisor is not a factor of the dividend (a.k.a. division with remainders) is often challenging for students. When problem situations involve *division with remainders*, students must make sense of the remainder and figure out its relationship to the other numbers in a solution strategy. It is also important that students get the chance to talk about the remainder as it appears in different symbolic expressions of the same situation. For example, consider the story problem featured in this activity (*Mrs. Lee has 50 popsicle sticks to divide among 6 groups of students. She will save any extra sticks for another project. How many sticks will each group get? How many will be left over?*) Solution strategies for this problem include both 50 ÷ 6 = 8 R 2 and 8 × 6 + 2 = 50. The first representation, 50 ÷ 6 = 8 R 2, focuses on the result of the division (i.e., the number of sticks given to each group) and records the remainder or leftover sticks separately. The second equation, 8 × 6 + 2 = 50, focuses on the equivalent relationship between the total number of sticks, 50, and the number of sticks in all the groups plus the 2 left over. Both representations reveal the same solution—6 groups with 8 sticks each and 2 sticks left over. Discussions in math class that focus on interpreting the numbers in each statement and the connections between them can help students develop a deep understanding of division with remainders.

Teaching Notes

1. Begin this activity by posting the popsicle stick story problem embedded in the activity. Ask students to solve the story problem.

2. Pass out Handout 1.4, *Division with Remainders*. Ask students to respond to the writing prompt on their own before talking with a partner. Listen in on students' conversations and use that information to help select speakers for the whole-class discussion. (See Step 3 for ideas on what to listen for.)

3. Call the class together for a whole-class discussion.

   a. Ask students to interpret each part of 50 ÷ 6 = 8 R 2. It is very important that students connect the expression 50 ÷ 6, the answer 8, and the symbols "R 2" to the problem context. Students should observe that 50 ÷ 6 can be interpreted as dividing or splitting 50 into 6 groups, 8 is the number of popsicle sticks given to each group, and "R 2" means that there will be 2 sticks left over.

   b. Because students often have difficulty interpreting remainders, be sure that all students can explain what the answer "8 R 2" means. You might ask, "So is each group getting '8 R 2' popsicle sticks? Is that what '8 R 2' means?" As you listen to students' answers, be sure that they understand that 8 R 2 is not a number. Instead, it is a statement that expresses two pieces of information—the size of each group plus the two leftover sticks. You may wish to draw a visual model that shows 8 groups of 6 and 2 left over. (See Figure. 1.8.)

Figure 1.8

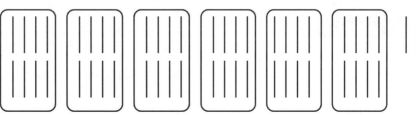

c. Next, talk about why the writer is confused about the equation
$6 \times 8 + 2 = 50$. Students should note that the writer is reading
$6 \times 8 + 2 = 50$ as equivalent to 6×10. In other words, he is adding
$8 + 2$ and multiplying the result by 6.

d. Talk about why this reasoning is flawed. Insist that students' reasoning goes deeper than simply referencing the order of operations.
Although students may say that the writer is wrong because
"according to order of operations, we multiply before we add,"
encourage them instead to think about the meaning of this equation
in the context of the problem. You might say, "What does 6×8
mean in this story?" (It means 6 groups of 8.) Then ask, "Why
does it make sense to add 2 to this product?" (Because after the
teacher gives 8 sticks to each of the 6 groups, there are 2 sticks left
over.) Ask students to connect the equation $6 \times 8 + 2 = 50$ to the
visual model created earlier in the discussion. (See Figure 1.8.)
Students should notice that, if we add the 6 groups of 8 sticks plus
the 2 leftover sticks, we get a total of 50 popsicle sticks. Use turn-
and-talk to give every student a chance to connect the equation
$6 \times 8 + 2 = 50$ to the story problem and to the visual model.

e. Connect the two representations, $50 \div 6 = 8$ R 2 and $6 \times 8 + 2 = 50$,
to each other. Ask students, "How are these two statements similar?
How are they different?" Students' observations may include the
following:

    i. The statements are similar because they both reveal the same
    information: each of the 6 groups gets 8 sticks with 2 sticks
    left over.

    ii. The statements are different because the division statement
    focuses on the result of the division—each group gets 8 sticks—
    and keeps the remainder or leftover, 2, separate. The other
    equation focuses on the equivalent relationship between the
    total number of sticks, 50, and the number of sticks in all the
    groups plus the two leftover, or extra, sticks.

4. Explain to students that, as they get older, they will be working
increasingly with equations that have more than one operation.
Reassure them that they can use what they know about each operation
to make sense of these equations.

5. Give students time to revisit their written answers so that they can
incorporate the ideas from the class discussion.

Extending the Activity

1. Post this story problem and the student solution that follows. Ask students to explain whether they think the solution is correct or incorrect.

*Nancy bought a large bag of 50 colored elastics. She needs 12
elastics to make a bracelet. How many bracelets can she make?*

One student's answer:
50 ÷ 12 = 4 R 2
4 + 2 = 6
Answer: 6 bracelets

(Possible response: The answer is incorrect because the student has added the quotient and the remainder. It does not make sense to add these two numbers because the quotient represents the number of bracelets and the remainder represents the leftover elastics. The correct answer to the story problem is 4 bracelets.)

2. Ask students to respond to the following writing prompt:

   If division is the opposite of multiplication, how do we rewrite division with remainders using multiplication? For example, if 121 ÷ 4 = 30 R 1, do we write 30 R 1 × 4 = 121? Why or why not?

   (Possible response: No, we should not write multiplication equations with remainders. When we divide, the divisor and the quotient are the factors in the related multiplication. The remainder can be added to the product of these two factors to form an expression equivalent to the dividend in the division equation. For example, since 121 ÷ 4 = 30 R 1, we can also write 4 × 30 + 1 = 121.)

3. Pose the following writing prompt to students:

   Imagine a student wrote 12 ÷ 3 = 4 R 0. Is this correct?

   (Possible response: This answer is correct. There is always a remainder after a division. The remainder is 0 when the divisor is a factor of the dividend. However, it is not required to write this remainder.)

Activity 1.5   Multiplying with Partial Products: Keeping Track of the Size of Each Factor

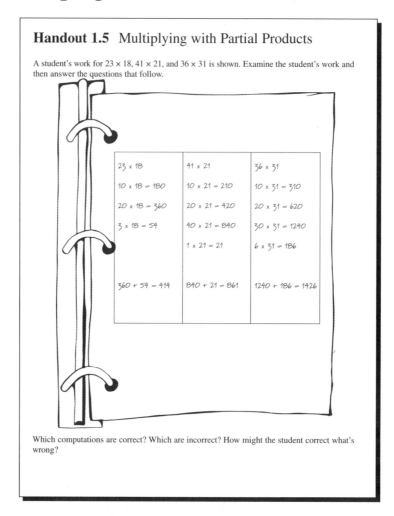

Handout 1.5 Multiplying with Partial Products

A student's work for 23 × 18, 41 × 21, and 36 × 31 is shown. Examine the student's work and then answer the questions that follow.

23 x 18	41 x 21	36 x 31
10 x 18 = 180	10 x 21 = 210	10 x 31 = 310
20 x 18 = 360	20 x 21 = 420	20 x 31 = 620
3 x 18 = 54	40 x 21 = 840	30 x 31 = 1240
	1 x 21 = 21	6 x 31 = 186
360 + 54 = 414	840 + 21 = 861	1240 + 186 = 1426

Which computations are correct? Which are incorrect? How might the student correct what's wrong?

Overview

This activity focuses on partial products as a strategy for multiplying two-digit numbers. Discussing the featured mistake will help students make an important distinction between doubling the result of a computation and combining multiples of ten.

Common Core Connections

Number and Operations in Base Ten, 4.B.5

Before You Use This Activity

Before you use this activity, be sure students have had prior experiences using partial products to multiply two-digit by one-digit numbers and two-digit by two-digit numbers. See, "Digging Deeper into the Math" for more information about partial products.

Materials (in Appendix)

Handout 1.5, *Multiplying with Partial Products*

Partial products offer an effective and efficient strategy for multiplying multi-digit numbers. With this strategy, at least one factor is split into smaller parts. The resulting parts are multiplied to create partial products. The partial products are added to find the product of the original computation. When partial products are used to multiply, it is often helpful to think about multiplication in terms of *equal groups*. For example, we can interpret the multiplication 23×18 as 23 groups of 18. Since the product of 23 groups of 18 is unknown, we might instead compute a friendlier partial product, such as 10 groups of 18. We can then double 180 to figure out that 20 groups of 18 is 360 ($20 \times 18 = 360$). Computing another 3 groups of 18 ($3 \times 18 = 54$) and adding the two partial products, 360 and 54, yields the final product, 414. This process can be modeled using an open array. (See Figure 1.9.)

Figure 1.9

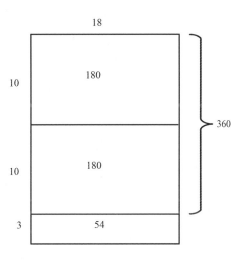

$$360 + 54 = 414$$

As students use partial products, they must attend carefully to the relationship between the number of groups and the size of the product. One common mistake occurs when students confuse adding ten groups with doubling. Because the product of $20 \times n$ is double the product of $10 \times n$, students may overgeneralize that adding another 10 groups of n to one product yields the same result as doubling that product. Talking about this error in class can help students understand that the product doubles only when the size of one factor doubles and can focus their attention on the difference between combining multiples of ten and doubling.

1. Before you pass out the handout, post the three computations embedded in the sample student work on the board and ask students to find the products using partial products.
2. Pass out Handout 1.5, *Multiplying with Partial Products.* Ask students to respond to the writing prompt on their own before talking with a

partner. Listen in on students' conversations and use that information to help select speakers for the whole-class discussion.

3. Call the class together for a whole-class discussion.

   a. Begin by asking students to talk about the three computations using the phrase *groups of*. (You may need to give an example, e.g., 23 × 18 can be thought of as 23 groups of 18.) Explain that even though we can interpret a multiplication computation in different ways, thinking of multiplication as *putting equal groups together* can be very helpful in making sense of computational strategies such as the one featured in this student work.

   b. Focus on the first computation, 23 × 18. Ask students to interpret the student's strategy and then explain any mistakes they found. Students should explain that the student is thinking about the computation as 20 × 18 plus 3 × 18. To find this product, the student computed 10 groups of 18 and doubled this product to find the product of 20 × 18. She found 3 groups of 18 and then added the two partial products to get the final answer, 414.

   c. Next, talk about the computation 41 × 21. Ask students to interpret the student's strategy and then explain whether they found any mistakes. Students should explain that the student is thinking about the computation as 40 groups of 21 plus 1 group of 21. The student finds 10 groups of 21 and doubles the product twice to find the product of 40 groups of 21. The student adds 1 group of 21 to 840 before adding the partial products, 840 and 21, to get the final product, 861.

   d. Before talking about the third computation, ask students to compare the first two computations. Students' observations should include the following:

      i.   Both use partial products by breaking the first factor into parts.
      ii. Both use multiplication by 10.
      iii. Both use the strategy of doubling one product to find another product.

   e. Talk about the third computation. Ask students to interpret the student's strategy and then explain any mistakes they found. Students should explain that the student is thinking about the computation as 36 groups of 31. The student begins by finding the product of 10 groups of 31. The student doubles this product to find the product of 20 groups of 31. The student doubles this product to find the product of 30 groups of 31, but this is not correct. If we double 20 groups of 31, we'd have 40 groups of 31, not 30.

      i.   Be sure to talk about why the student might have made this mistake. For example, students might note that the doubling strategy worked correctly in the two previous problems. Perhaps the student assumed it would work for all examples.

    ii. Talk about how to fix the mistake. Students might suggest adding the products of 10 × 31 and 20 × 31 to find the product of 30 × 31. Then, the student can add six more groups of 31 to reach the final product of 1116. Students might also suggest tripling the product 10 × 31 to find 30 × 31 before adding on the final six groups of 31; 930 + 186 = 1116.

4. Give students time to revise their written answers so that they can incorporate the ideas from the class discussion.

Extending the Activity

1. Post the sample student work. Ask students to find and correct the mistakes.

41 x 21	26 x 31	23 x 19
41 x 10 = 410	26 x 10 = 260	23 x 10 = 230
41 x 20 = 820	26 x 20 = 520	23 x 3 = 69
41 x 1 = 41	26 x 30 = 1040	23 x 6 = 138
	26 x 1 = 26	23 x 9 = 276
820 + 41 = 861	1040 + 26 = 1066	230 + 276 = 506

(Possible response: The work for the first computation is correct. The student used the partial products 41 × 20 and 41 × 1 to find the product of 41 × 21. The work for the second computation is not correct. The student doubled the product of 26 × 20 to find the product of 26 × 30. This is not correct; we can only double the product if one factor doubles. The student can fix this error by adding the products of 26 × 10 and 26 × 20 to find 26 × 30; 260 + 520 = 780. The student can add the product of 26 × 1 to reach the final answer of 806. The third computation is also not correct. The student doubled the product of 23 × 6 to find 23 × 9. This is not correct, however, because 9 is not two times 6. The student can correct this error by adding the products of 23 × 3 and 23 × 6; 69 + 138 = 207. The corrected strategy would read: (23 × 10) + (23 × 9) = 230 + 207 = 437.)

2. Post the sample student work. Ask students to find and correct the mistakes.

23 x 19	31 x 29	19 x 24
23 x 20 = 460	31 x 30 = 930	20 x 24 = 480
460 - 23 = 437	930 - 31 = 899	480 - 19 = 461

(Possible response: The first and second computations are correct. In both problems, the student increased the second factor by one to create easier computations. The student then subtracts an amount equal to what was added in order to find the product of the original computation. For example, we can compute 23 groups of 19 using the product of 23 × 20. Because we increased each of the 23 groups by 1, we need to subtract 23 from the product of 23 × 20; 460 – 23 = 437. The third computation is not correct. The student tried to find the product of 19 × 24 using the friendlier computation 20 × 24, or 20 groups of 24. Then, the student subtracted 19. This is not correct. Changing 19 × 24 to 20 × 24 adds another group of 24 to the product. So, the student needs to subtract 24 from the product of 20 × 24; 480 – 24 = 456.)

Activity 1.6   Dividing with Partial Quotients: Making Decisions About How to Partition the Dividend

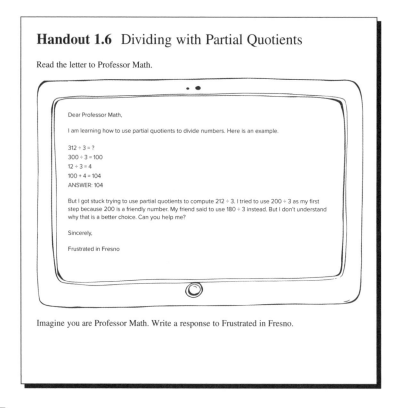

Handout 1.6 Dividing with Partial Quotients

Read the letter to Professor Math.

Dear Professor Math,

I am learning how to use partial quotients to divide numbers. Here is an example.

312 ÷ 3 = ?
300 ÷ 3 = 100
12 ÷ 3 = 4
100 + 4 = 104
ANSWER: 104

But I got stuck trying to use partial quotients to compute 212 ÷ 3. I tried to use 200 ÷ 3 as my first step because 200 is a friendly number. My friend said to use 180 ÷ 3 instead. But I don't understand why that is a better choice. Can you help me?

Sincerely,

Frustrated in Fresno

Imagine you are Professor Math. Write a response to Frustrated in Fresno.

Overview

In this activity, students play the role of Professor Math and offer advice to a writer who is confused about using partial quotients as a strategy for dividing whole numbers. Talking about the featured mistake helps students think deeply about the meaning of the divisor and quotient in a division computation as well as the relationship between them.

Common Core Connections

Number and Operations in Base Ten, 4.B.6

Before You Use This Activity

Before you use this activity, students should have had prior experiences using multiples of ten to compute quotients. For example, we can find 280 ÷ 4 using 28 ÷ 4 = 7. We can interpret 280 ÷ 4 as 28 tens divided by 4; 280 ÷ 4 = 70 (or 7 tens).

Materials (in Appendix)

Handout 1.6, *Dividing with Partial Quotients*

Digging Deeper into the Math

The strategy of partial quotients offers students an efficient and effective way to divide whole numbers. To use this strategy effectively, students must make a sound decision about how to partition the dividend. The criteria for making this decision are often more complicated for division than for other operations. Students must think carefully about how to partition the dividend into friendly numbers that are also multiples of the divisor. For example, when dividing 212 ÷ 3, students may be tempted to partition 212 into 200 and 12 because 200 is a friendly number. This is not an easy computation, however, because 200 is not a multiple of 3. Figuring out the number of groups of 3 in 200 is not easy. A better choice is to partition 212 into 180 plus 32 because 180 is both a multiple of 10 (also known as a friendly number) and a multiple of 3. We can compute 180 ÷ 3 by thinking about the number of groups of 3 in 180 (180 ÷ 3 = 60). We continue by thinking about the number of groups of 3 in 32. Again, students should look for a friendly number that is close to 32 and also a multiple of 3. A good choice is 30 because 30 ÷ 3 = 10. We now add the total number of groups, 60 + 10 = 70, and record this—along with the leftover, or remainder, 2—as the solution 70 R 2. Figure 1.10 shows a geometric model for this strategy.

Figure 1.10

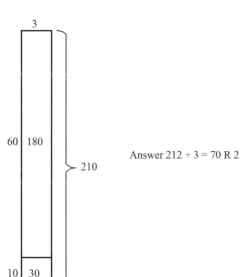

212 ÷ 3   "How many groups of 3 are in 212?"

180 + 30 + 2

Answer 212 ÷ 3 = 70 R 2

Teaching Notes

1. Begin the discussion by asking students to perform the computations featured in the letter to Professor Math.
2. Pass out Handout 1.6, *Dividing with Partial Quotients*. Ask students to respond to the writing prompt on their own before talking with a partner. Listen in on students' conversations and use that information to help you select speakers for the whole-class discussion. (See Step 3 for ideas you might listen for.)
3. Call the class together for a whole-class discussion.
   a. Talk about how we can interpret the division 312 ÷ 3. Be sure that students can interpret this computation in terms of the repeated subtraction or measurement interpretation of division (i.e., the number of groups of 3 in 312) before continuing.

Figure 1.11

b. Ask students to think about why the student might have used 300 ÷ 3 to find the quotient. For example, students might note that 300 ÷ 3 is a friendly computation.

c. Ask students to explain the next step in the procedure and to connect both steps to the final answer.

d. Ask students to describe how we could draw an array to represent this strategy. One possible array is shown in Figure 1.11. Ask students to identify the remainder. Students should respond that the remainder is 0 because 312 is a multiple of 3.

e. Now focus on the computation 212 ÷ 3. Generate possible reasons the writer might want to use 200 ÷ 3 as the first step. For example, the writer may have chosen this step because 200 is a friendly number. It may seem like 200 is a good choice because, often, multiples of 100 are easy to work with.

f. Ask students to assess whether 200 really is a helpful choice for partitioning the dividend. Students should respond that 200 is not particularly helpful for this computation because 200 is not a multiple of 3; it's not easy to compute 200 ÷ 3.

g. Ask students to assess whether 180 is a helpful choice for partitioning the dividend. Students should respond that yes, 180 is a helpful choice because 180 is a multiple of 3. It is also 10 times greater than 18, so we can figure out 180 ÷ 3 easily (180 ÷ 3 = 60).

h. Ask the students to complete the computation. What might they do after computing 180 ÷ 3 = 60? Students can either show the steps with an open array (as in Figure 1.10) or numerically as follows:

    180 ÷ 3 = 60
    212 – 180 = 32
    32 ÷ 3 = 10 R 2
    60 + 10 = 70
    Answer: 70 R 2

i. Summarize the discussion by explaining that when we use partial quotients to divide, it helps to choose numbers that are both friendly (e.g., multiples of 100) and multiples of the divisor.

4. Ask students to revisit their original responses so that they can include information gleaned during the whole-class discussion.

Extending the Activity

1. Show students the computation 341 ÷ 8 and pose the following problem:

    Imagine a friend tried to compute the quotient using partial quotients. The friend split 341 into 300 + 41. Is this a good choice? Why or why not?

    (Possible response: For this computation, 300 and 41 are not friendly partitions because 300 is not a multiple of 8. It is not easy to find the number of groups of 8 in 300. A better choice is 320 and 21 because

320 is a multiple of 8; 320 ÷ 8 = 40 and 21 ÷ 8 = 2 R 5. The quotient is 42 R 5.)

2. Ask students to determine what went wrong with the student's strategy (see following equation).

204 ÷ 3

100 ÷ 3 = 33 R 1

100 ÷ 3 = 33 R 1

4 ÷ 3 = 1 R 1

Answer: 67 R 3

(Possible response: The student did not take the three leftover ones and form another group of 3. The quotient should be 68.)

Activity 1.7　Dividing with Two-Digit Dividends: Using Division by 10 to Compute Other Quotients

Handout 1.7 Dividing with Two-Digit Dividends

Read the comic. Then answer the questions that follows.

Questions:
1. Why did DA compute 480 ÷ 10 as the first step in his strategy?
2. Why does DA think it makes sense to compute 48 × 3 as his second step?
3. Does DA's second step, 48 × 3, make sense? Why or why not?

Overview

The mathematical focus of this lesson is division with a two-digit divisor that is a multiple of ten. The student in the comic uses 480 ÷ 10 to compute 480 ÷ 30. The student makes a mistake when she triples the quotient of 480 ÷ 10 (48) instead of dividing it by three. By reading the comic strip and talking about the discussion questions that follow, students get a chance to think deeply about the relationship between the size of the divisor and the size of the dividend in a multidigit division computation.

Common Core Connections

Number and Operations in Base Ten, 5.B.6

Before You Use This Activity

Before using this activity in your classroom, students should have had prior experience working with multiplication and division with multiples of ten.

Materials (in Appendix)

Handout 1.7, *Dividing with Two-Digit Dividends*

Digging Deeper into the Math

This activity focuses on the strategy of using division by 10 to work with divisors that are multiples of 10. The activity focuses on the computation 480 ÷ 30, which can be interpreted in terms of repeated subtraction or measurement (i.e., the number of groups of 30 in 480). Given that 30 is a multiple of 10, it may be helpful to compute 480 ÷ 30 using the related expression 480 ÷ 10. We can read 480 ÷ 10 as the number of groups of 10 in 480. Counting by tens (or thinking about the number of tens per hundred), we can reason that 480 ÷ 10 = 48. We know that 30 is three times 10, but does that mean we should multiply 48 by 3 or divide 48 by 3? Comparing 480 ÷ 10 to 480 ÷ 30, we can see that the size of the groups has grown by a factor of 3. Since the groups are three times as big, the total number of groups must be three times smaller—or reduced by a factor of 3. In other words, because there are now three tens in each group (instead of one), there must be three times fewer groups. This tells us that the quotient of 480 ÷ 30 is *one-third* the quotient of 480 ÷ 10. A base 10 model (e.g., base 10 blocks) provides a useful model for illustrating these ideas. (See Figure 1.12.)

Figure 1.12

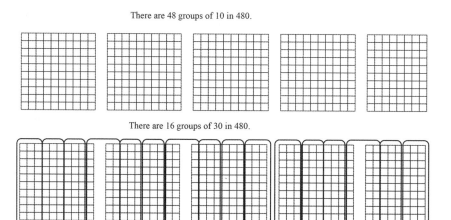

There are 48 groups of 10 in 480.

There are 16 groups of 30 in 480.

Alternatively, we can interpret the computation $480 \div 30$ in terms of the partitive or equal groupings interpretation of division (i.e., 480 is divided into 30 groups). The related computation $480 \div 10 = 48$ tells us that when 480 is divided into 10 groups, the size of each group is 48. If we want to create three times as many groups, we need to make each group three times as small. This tells us that we need to divide 48 by 3 in order to find the size of each of the 30 groups.

$480 \div 30 = ?$
$480 \div 10 = 48$
$48 \div 3 = 16$
$480 \div 30 = 16$

Teaching Notes

1. Pass out Handout 1.7, *Dividing with Two-Digit Dividends*. You may decide to have students read the comic as a script or even act it out. Or you may ask students to read the comic silently on their own and then describe it in their own words.

2. Give students time to work through the discussion questions either on their own or with a partner before talking about them as a whole class.

3. Call the students together for a whole-class discussion.

   a. First, address why the student might have computed $480 \div 30$ using $480 \div 10$. Students should note that dividing by 10 is easier than dividing by 30.

   b. Generate possible reasons the student might have taken the quotient of $480 \div 10$ (48) and multiplied it by 3 to compute $480 \div 30$. For example, perhaps the student reasoned that the quotient should be 3 times 48 because 30 is 3 times 10.

   c. Ask students to explain why this choice is wrong. Students may use the equal groupings interpretation of division to explain that $480 \div 30$ can be thought of as 480 divided into 30 groups. If we compute $480 \div 10$, we have divided 480 into 10 groups with 48 in each group. If we multiply 48 by 3, that would mean that we are tripling the size of the groups. But we don't want to do that. We want to create three times as many groups. Or, students might use the repeated subtraction interpretation of division to explain that tripling the size of the groups from 10 to 30 would not also triple the number of the groups.

   d. Ask what the student should do after he computes $480 \div 10$. Students may reason that he should divide 48 by 3 by referring to equal groupings. Because we need to make three times as many groups, we need to reduce the size of the groups by a factor of 3. Or, using repeated subtraction, since we need to make the groups three times as large, we will have only 3 times fewer groups. Record this symbolically as follows:

$$480 \div 30 = ?$$
$$480 \div 10 = 48$$
$$48 \div 3 = 16$$
$$480 \div 30 = 16$$

4. Ask students to revisit their original responses so that they can include information gleaned during the whole-class discussion.

Extending the Activity

1. Pose the following problem:

    Imagine a student divides 360 ÷ 40 by computing 360 ÷ 10 = 36. She then gets stuck because she doesn't know whether to multiply 36 by 4 or divide 36 by 4. What should she do?

    (Possible response: The student should divide 36 by 4. The total number of groups of 40 in 360 will be four times smaller than the total number of groups of 10 in 360. The bigger the size of each group, the smaller the number of groups that can be made. Since groups of 40 are four times bigger than groups of 10, we can make four times fewer groups; 36 ÷ 4 = 9.)

2. Pose the following problem:

    Imagine a student divides 240 ÷ 15 by computing 240 ÷ 3 = 80. He then gets stuck because he doesn't know whether to multiply 80 by 5 or to divide 80 by 5. What should he do?

    (Possible response: The student should divide 80 by 5. The total number of groups of 15 will be five times smaller than the total number of groups of 3 in 240. The bigger the size of each group, the smaller the number of groups that can be made. Since groups of 15 are five times bigger than groups of 3, we can make five times fewer groups; 80 ÷ 5 = 16.)

Chapter 2

Fractions

Fractions are a focal point of students' arithmetical work in grades four and five. During these grades, students solve problems that involve multiple interpretations of fractions, extend and adapt ideas about whole numbers to the set of rational numbers, and learn how to operate on fractions and mixed numbers. Students' mistakes with fractions stem from a variety of sources, including misidentifying the unit, using computational procedures they don't understand, and forming faulty overgeneralizations (e.g., that bigger numerals signal bigger fractions). The activities in this chapter address these mistakes while also drawing students' attention toward important concepts and relationships that define a strong sense of rational number.

Activity 2.1   Working with Unit Fractions: Connecting One-Fourth to One Whole

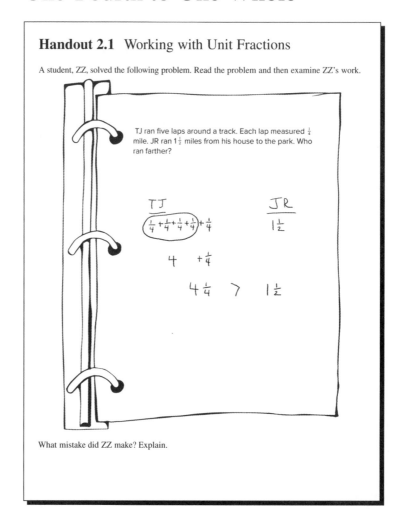

Handout 2.1 Working with Unit Fractions

A student, ZZ, solved the following problem. Read the problem and then examine ZZ's work.

TJ ran five laps around a track. Each lap measured $\frac{1}{4}$ mile. JR ran $1\frac{1}{2}$ miles from his house to the park. Who ran farther?

TJ

$\boxed{\frac{1}{4}+\frac{1}{4}+\frac{1}{4}+\frac{1}{4}}+\frac{1}{4}$

JR

$1\frac{1}{2}$

$4 \quad +\frac{1}{4}$

$4\frac{1}{4} \quad > \quad 1\frac{1}{2}$

What mistake did ZZ make? Explain.

Overview

In this activity, students examine a common mistake related to adding a set of unit fractions. Students examine a piece of student work that shows the mistake $\frac{1}{4} + \frac{1}{4} + \frac{1}{4} + \frac{1}{4} = 4$. Discussing the error provides students with an opportunity to think carefully about the equivalent relationship between four groups of $\frac{1}{4}$ and the whole number 1. It also encourages students to think deeply about the importance of the size of the piece as well as the number of pieces when adding fractions.

Common Core Connections

Number and Operations—Fractions, 4.B.3

Before You Use This Activity

Students should have had prior experience counting by unit fractions (e.g., $\frac{1}{4}, \frac{2}{4}, \frac{3}{4}, \frac{4}{4}, \frac{5}{4}$) and finding equivalent fractions using unit fractions (e.g., $\frac{1}{4} + \frac{1}{4}$ $= \frac{2}{4} = \frac{1}{2}$) before working on this task.

Materials (in Appendix)

Handout 2.1, *Working with Unit Fractions*

Digging Deeper into the Math

This activity focuses on miscalculating the sum of a set of unit fractions. In the activity, a student incorrectly concludes that the sum of $\frac{1}{4} + \frac{1}{4} + \frac{1}{4} + \frac{1}{4}$ is 4 instead of 1. As elementary students begin to operate on, compare, and reason about fractions, they may focus on counting parts without regard to size. If students count the sum of $\frac{1}{4} + \frac{1}{4} + \frac{1}{4} + \frac{1}{4}$ as 4, they may be counting the number of parts without attending to the size of those parts. Talking about why $\frac{1}{4} + \frac{1}{4} + \frac{1}{4} + \frac{1}{4}$ is not equal to 4 (even though we are adding four "copies" of $\frac{1}{4}$) is one way to help students attend to both the number of parts and the size of the parts when they reason about fractions and record sums using fraction notation.

Teaching Notes

1. Post the word problem embedded in this task on the board. Ask students to solve the word problem on their own.

2. Pass out Handout 2.1, *Working with Unit Fractions*. Ask students to examine the student work and respond to the writing prompt on their own before sharing their ideas with a partner. As students talk, listen in on their conversations to help you choose speakers for the whole-class discussion. (See Step 3 for key ideas to listen for.)

3. Pull the class together for a whole-class discussion.

   a. Focus the whole-class discussion on why ZZ may have written that $\frac{1}{4} + \frac{1}{4} + \frac{1}{4} + \frac{1}{4} = 4$. As students share their ideas, be sure to focus on the idea that ZZ is counting parts. ZZ may have reasoned that there are four $\frac{1}{4}$s in the expression $\frac{1}{4} + \frac{1}{4} + \frac{1}{4} + \frac{1}{4}$. Then, talk about why it is incorrect to reason that $\frac{1}{4} + \frac{1}{4} + \frac{1}{4} + \frac{1}{4} = 4$. You might ask, "So if there are four parts when we add $\frac{1}{4} + \frac{1}{4} + \frac{1}{4} + \frac{1}{4}$, why isn't the sum equal to 4?" As students share ideas, be sure they address the size of the parts. Even though there are four parts, each part is one-fourth of a whole, so we must show this when we record the answer.

   b. As you talk about the equivalence $\frac{1}{4} + \frac{1}{4} + \frac{1}{4} + \frac{1}{4} = \frac{4}{4} = 1$, spend time unpacking and connecting the parts of this relationship. First, be sure students can *read* the symbol $\frac{4}{4}$ as four-fourths and explain what this means (e.g., four $\frac{1}{4}$s or four copies of $\frac{1}{4}$). Second, talk about why four $\frac{1}{4}$s are equal to 1 (e.g., four parts out of four parts is the same as one whole).

   c. After discussing what is wrong with ZZ's strategy, spend some time talking about how to fix the error so that ZZ might find the correct solution. Students may suggest that ZZ should record the sum of $\frac{1}{4} + \frac{1}{4} + \frac{1}{4} + \frac{1}{4}$ as 1. This tells ZZ that TJ ran $1\frac{1}{4}$ miles. Then ZZ can compare $1\frac{1}{4}$ to $1\frac{1}{2}$ by noting that $\frac{1}{4}$ is less than $\frac{1}{2}$ (since $\frac{2}{4} = \frac{1}{2}$). So, JR ran farther than TJ.

4. Following this discussion, ask students to revise and add on to their original responses to incorporate the ideas they talked about during the whole-class discussion.

Extending the Activity

1. Post the same story problem embedded in the original task and the sample student work presented here. Ask students to find and correct the mistake.

TJ:

5 laps

$\frac{1}{4}$ mile each lap

$\frac{1}{4} + \frac{1}{4} + \frac{1}{4} + \frac{1}{4} + \frac{1}{4} = 5\frac{1}{4}$

$5\frac{1}{4} > 1\frac{1}{2}$ so TJ ran farther

JR:

$1\frac{1}{2}$ miles

(Possible response: The student wrote the sum of five groups of $\frac{1}{4}$ as the mixed number $5\frac{1}{4}$. This is incorrect. Four groups of $\frac{1}{4}$ equal 1. If we add one more $\frac{1}{4}$, we get a total of one and one-fourth, or $1\frac{1}{4}$. This can also be written symbolically as $\frac{1}{4} + \frac{1}{4} + \frac{1}{4} + \frac{1}{4} + \frac{1}{4} = 1 + \frac{1}{4} = 1\frac{1}{4}$.

2. Pose the following problem to students:

Imagine the following question appeared on a quiz:

Compare $\frac{4}{3}$ and $4\frac{1}{3}$ using <, >, or =.

Imagine a friend wrote $\frac{4}{3} = 4\frac{1}{3}$ because "both numbers mean 'four one-thirds.'"

What do you think about this answer?

(Possible response: Only the first fraction, $\frac{4}{3}$, can be interpreted as four one-thirds or four groups of one-third or one and one-third. The mixed number, $4\frac{1}{3}$, means 4 and one-third or 4 wholes plus another one-third.

Activity 2.2 Comparing Fractions: Coordinating the Size of Each Piece and the Number of Pieces

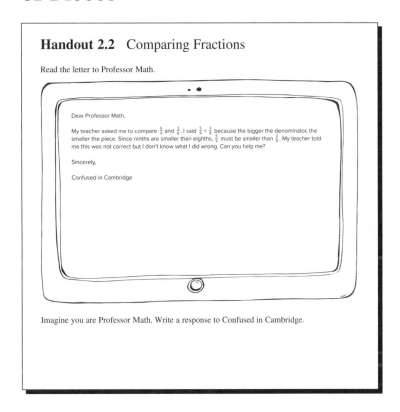

Handout 2.2 Comparing Fractions

Read the letter to Professor Math.

Dear Professor Math,

My teacher asked me to compare $\frac{5}{9}$ and $\frac{3}{8}$. I said $\frac{5}{9} < \frac{3}{8}$ because the bigger the denominator, the smaller the piece. Since ninths are smaller than eighths, $\frac{5}{9}$ must be smaller than $\frac{3}{8}$. My teacher told me this was not correct but I don't know what I did wrong. Can you help me?

Sincerely,

Confused in Cambridge

Imagine you are Professor Math. Write a response to Confused in Cambridge.

Overview

This activity addresses strategies for comparing fractions. The highlighted mistake focuses on misusing the generalization that *the bigger the denominator, the smaller the piece* to compare two fractions with different numerators. Students will read the letter to Professor Math, talk about why the comparison strategy is not helpful for this particular pair of factions, and write a response to the confused student from the perspective of Professor Math.

Common Core Connections

Number and Operations—Fractions, 4.A.2

Before You Use This Activity

Before using this activity in your classroom, be sure students have had prior experiences finding equivalent fractions for one-half.

Materials (in Appendix)

Handout 2.2, *Comparing Fractions*

Digging Deeper into the Math

As they progress through the upper elementary grades, students learn a set of strategies for comparing fractions. For example, students may learn to compare fractions by comparing denominators (e.g., $\frac{3}{8} < \frac{3}{7}$ because eighths are smaller than sevenths) and comparing numerators (e.g., $\frac{3}{8} < \frac{5}{8}$ because 3 is less than 5). When the numerators and denominators of two fractions are both different, an effective strategy is *compare to one-half*. For example, we can compare $\frac{5}{9}$ and $\frac{3}{8}$ by comparing each fraction to $\frac{1}{2}$. Since half of 9 is $4\frac{1}{2}$, we know $\frac{5}{9} > \frac{1}{2}$. Since half of 8 is 4, we know $\frac{3}{8} < \frac{1}{2}$. We use this information to conclude that $\frac{5}{9} > \frac{3}{8}$.

To use fraction comparison strategies correctly, students need to understand the characteristics of numbers that lend themselves to one strategy over another. For example, it makes sense to compare $\frac{3}{8}$ and $\frac{3}{7}$ by comparing denominators because their numerators are the same. By contrast, this strategy would not be appropriate for $\frac{5}{9}$ and $\frac{3}{8}$ because these fractions have different numerators and denominators. Instead, a better choice for comparing these fractions is *compare to one-half* because one fraction is less than one-half and the other is greater.

Teaching Notes

1. Post the two fractions $\frac{5}{9}$ and $\frac{3}{8}$ on the board and ask students to compare them using $<$, $>$, or $=$. Ask students to turn and talk with a partner about their comparison strategies.

2. Pass out Handout 2.2, *Comparing Fractions*. Ask students to examine the student work and respond to the writing prompt on their own before sharing their ideas with a partner. As students talk, listen in on their conversations to help you choose speakers for the whole-class discussion. (See Step 3 for key ideas to listen for.)

3. Pull the class together for a whole-class discussion.

    a. Ask students to describe what the writer means by *the bigger the denominator, the smaller the piece*. Students may explain that as the unit or whole gets divided into more and more pieces, the size of those pieces becomes smaller and smaller.

    b. Ask students to think about why the writer is using the idea that *the bigger the denominator, the smaller the piece* as a fraction comparison strategy. Students may respond that this idea can often be used as a strategy for comparing fractions. For example, we can use it to compare $\frac{5}{9}$ and $\frac{5}{8}$ or $\frac{3}{9}$ and $\frac{3}{8}$. This strategy is most helpful when the numerators are the same.

    c. Ask students if the idea that *the bigger the denominator, the smaller the piece* helps to compare $\frac{3}{8}$ and $\frac{5}{9}$. Students should notice that the strategy is not helpful here. Since $\frac{3}{8}$ and $\frac{5}{9}$ have different numerators, we can't use *the bigger the denominator, the smaller the piece* to say that $\frac{5}{9}$ is smaller than $\frac{3}{8}$. Even though ninths are smaller than eighths, $\frac{5}{9}$ has more pieces than $\frac{3}{8}$.

    d. Ask students to describe a strategy that will help us make an accurate comparison. Students may suggest the strategy *compare to one-half*. Since half of 9 is $4\frac{1}{2}$, we know that $\frac{5}{9}$ is greater than $\frac{1}{2}$. Since half of 8 is 4, we know $\frac{3}{8}$ is less than $\frac{1}{2}$. This tells us that $\frac{5}{9} > \frac{3}{8}$.)

4. Following this discussion, ask students to revise and add on to their original responses to incorporate the ideas they talked about during the whole-class discussion.

Extending the Activity

1. Pose the following question to students:

   NC thinks that $\frac{7}{16}$ is greater than $\frac{5}{9}$ because 7 is greater than 5. Is his reasoning correct?

   (Possible response: No, NC's reasoning is not correct. When comparing fractions, we need to consider the entire fraction as one number. In this case, it also helps to compare each number to one-half. Since $\frac{7}{16}$ is less than $\frac{1}{2}$ and $\frac{5}{9}$ is greater than $\frac{1}{2}$, $\frac{7}{16} < \frac{5}{9}$).

2. Pose the following question to students:

   CZ thinks that $\frac{3}{7}$ is equal to $\frac{5}{11}$ because they each need just half of another piece to equal one-half. What is wrong with CZ's reasoning?

   (Possible response: Even though each fraction needs *just half of another piece* to equal $\frac{1}{2}$, the additional piece needed is larger for $\frac{3}{7}$ than $\frac{5}{11}$. We need to add half of $\frac{1}{7}$ to $\frac{3}{7}$ but only half of $\frac{1}{11}$ to $\frac{5}{11}$. Because we need to add a smaller piece to $\frac{5}{11}$ to get to $\frac{1}{2}$, $\frac{3}{7} < \frac{5}{11}$).

Activity 2.3   Adding Fractions: Splitting One Addend into Parts

Handout 2.3 Adding Fractions

Read the comic. Then answer the question that follows.

If you were a student in this class, how would you respond to the teacher's question?

Overview

This activity focuses on adding mixed numbers by decomposing (or splitting) one of the addends in parts. The featured mistake involves changing the value of the addend in the process of decomposing (or splitting) it into parts. After reading the comic strip, students talk about the importance of maintaining the value of the addend when we decompose (or split) it into parts.

Common Core Connections

Number and Operations—Fractions, 5.A.1

Before You Use This Activity

Before you use this activity, students should have had experience adding fractions with unlike denominators.

Materials (in Appendix)

Handout 2.3, *Adding Fractions*

Adding two numbers by decomposing one addend into parts is an effective way to add whole numbers, fractions, and decimals. This strategy is particularly helpful when modeled on the open number line. For example, to add $2\frac{5}{6} + 1\frac{1}{3}$, we locate $2\frac{5}{6}$ on the number line and add on $1\frac{1}{3}$ units in smaller, friendlier parts. The answer, or sum, is the location where we land. (See Figure 2.1.)

Figure 2.1

When students use this strategy, they must make sure that they do not change the total value of the second addend in the process of splitting it into parts. In the previous example, students can get confused about how much more to add on after they have added $\frac{1}{6}$ and 1. As seen in the comic strip that follows, students may add on another $\frac{1}{3}$ because the fraction in the mixed number, $1\frac{1}{3}$, is $\frac{1}{3}$. Students need to realize, however, that because they already added $\frac{1}{6}$, only $\frac{1}{6}$ remains to be added. The correct sum is $4\frac{1}{6}$. (*Note*: An open number line does not show all tick marks and does not require that locations be proportionally accurate; e.g., a distance of $\frac{1}{3}$ should be longer than a distance of $\frac{1}{6}$ but need not be twice as long.)

1. Before students read the comic strip, ask them to add $2\frac{5}{6} + 1\frac{1}{3}$. Encourage them to try to find the sum using two different strategies.

2. Pass out Handout 2.3, *Adding Fractions*. Ask students to respond to the writing prompt on their own before turning and talking with a partner about their ideas. As students talk, listen in on their conversations and use that information to decide who to call on later when you talk as a whole class. (See Step 3 for key ideas to listen for.)

3. Pull the class together for a whole-class discussion.
   a. First, ask students to describe MJ's strategy. Be sure students' descriptions focus on the fact that MJ is adding $2\frac{5}{6} + 1\frac{1}{3}$ by adding $1\frac{1}{3}$ in friendlier parts.
   b. Next, ask students to think about why MJ might have added $\frac{1}{3}$ to 4 and to explain why this is wrong. Students may respond that MJ might think he should add $\frac{1}{3}$ because the second number in the computation is $1\frac{1}{3}$. Since he has just added 1, he might think it makes sense now to add $\frac{1}{3}$. This is not correct because MJ has already added $1\frac{1}{6}$. If he adds another $\frac{1}{3}$, he has added more than $1\frac{1}{3}$.

c. Ask students what MJ can do to correct his error. Students might suggest that MJ should think about how much he has left to add in order to add a total of $1\frac{1}{3}$. Since he added $\frac{1}{6}$ as his first step and $\frac{1}{6} + \frac{1}{6} = \frac{1}{3}$, MJ needs to add another $\frac{1}{6}$.

4. Following this discussion, ask students to revise and add on to their original responses to incorporate the ideas they talked about during the whole-class discussion.

Extending the Activity

1. Post the student work. Ask students to describe and correct the errors that they see.

$4\frac{1}{3} + 1\frac{2}{3} = ?$	$1\frac{2}{3} + 2\frac{2}{3} = ?$	$4\frac{3}{4} + 2\frac{1}{2} = ?$
$4\frac{1}{3} + \frac{2}{3} = 5$	$1\frac{2}{3} + \frac{2}{3} = 2$	$4\frac{3}{4} + \frac{1}{2} = 5$
$5 + 1 = 6$	$2 + 2 = 4$	$5 + 2 = 7$
	$4 + \frac{2}{3} = 4\frac{2}{3}$	

(Possible response: The first computation is correct. The student maintained the value of the addend when she split it into parts. The second and third computations are not correct. When the student split each of these addends into parts, she did not maintain the value of the addend. The student can fix the second computation by changing the steps to $1\frac{2}{3} + \frac{1}{3} = 2$; $2 + 2 = 4$; $4 + \frac{1}{3} = 4\frac{1}{3}$. The student can fix the third computation by changing the steps to $4\frac{3}{4} + \frac{1}{4} = 5$; $5 + 2 = 7$; $7 + \frac{1}{4} = 7\frac{1}{4}$.)

2. Post the student work. Ask students to describe and fix the errors that they see.

$5\frac{2}{3} + 8\frac{2}{3}$	$4\frac{4}{5} + 7\frac{2}{5}$	$9\frac{3}{4} + 3\frac{3}{8}$
$5\frac{2}{3} + \frac{1}{3} = 6$	$4\frac{4}{5} + \frac{1}{5} = 5$	$9\frac{3}{4} + \frac{1}{4} = 10$
$6 + 8 = 14$	$5 + 7 = 12$	$10 + 3 = 13$
$14 + \frac{1}{3} = 14\frac{1}{3}$	$12 + \frac{1}{5} = 12\frac{1}{5}$	$13 + \frac{2}{8} = 13 + \frac{1}{4} = 13\frac{1}{4}$

(Possible response: The first and second computations are correct. The student breaks the second addend in each computation into three friendlier pieces. The third computation is not correct; the value of the second addend is changed when it is broken into friendlier pieces. The student adds $\frac{1}{4}$ to $9\frac{3}{4}$ to create a whole-number partial sum. Then the student adds $10 + 3 = 13$, which is also correct. But then the student adds $\frac{2}{8}$, which is not correct. Because the original addend was $3\frac{3}{8}$, and the student has already added 3 and $\frac{1}{4}$, the student should add $\frac{1}{8}$. The final step should be changed as follows: $13 + \frac{1}{8} = 13\frac{1}{8}$.

Activity 2.4 Subtracting Fractions: What Does It Mean to "Check Your Work"?

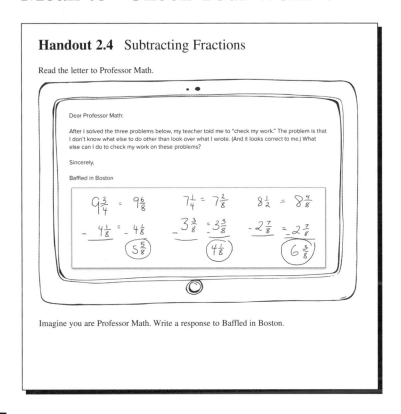

Handout 2.4 Subtracting Fractions

Read the letter to Professor Math.

Dear Professor Math:

After I solved the three problems below, my teacher told me to "check my work." The problem is that I don't know what else to do other than look over what I wrote. (And it looks correct to me.) What else can I do to check my work on these problems?

Sincerely,

Baffled in Boston

Imagine you are Professor Math. Write a response to Baffled in Boston.

Overview

In this activity, students write a response to a writer who is confused about what it means to *check your work*. The writer provides three mixed number subtraction computations and asks Professor Math for advice on checking his work. The featured mistake focuses on subtracting the smaller fraction from the bigger fraction without regard to its position within the overall expression. Students are asked to write a response to the writer that suggests checking his work and how to use those strategies to find and correct the mistakes.

Common Core Connections

Number and Operations—Fractions, 5.A.1

Before You Use This Activity

Before you use this activity in class, students should have had prior experience subtracting fractions and mixed numbers with unlike denominators.

Materials (in Appendix)

Handout 2.4, *Subtracting Fractions*

Digging Deeper into the Math

This activity features a common mistake with subtracting mixed numbers. The fictitious student subtracts the smaller fraction from the bigger fraction without considering its position within the computation. For example, he finds the incorrect difference for $7\frac{1}{4} - 3\frac{3}{8}$ when he subtracts $\frac{1}{4}$ from $\frac{3}{8}$. One way to help students correct this mistake is to encourage them to model the subtraction on a number line. (See "Teaching Notes" for examples of number line models.) It may also help to use a different interpretation of subtraction to read the expression. For example, if the student thinks of the expression as $3\frac{3}{8} + ? = 7\frac{1}{4}$, he can add on to $3\frac{3}{8}$ to find the correct difference.

Teaching Notes

1. You may wish to begin this activity with a brief discussion about why teachers always say, "Check your work." After students share their own ideas, here are a few ideas you may want to share as well:
   a. Effective problem solvers spend a lot of time looking for mistakes in their solution strategies.
   b. When they reach the end of a solution strategy, effective problem solvers tend to assume they made at least one mistake and become detectives trying to find what they did wrong.
   c. It is *not* true that good problem solvers make fewer mistakes.
2. Explain to students that what you do to check your work depends on what kind of math problem you are working on. For example, what students do to check their work on a subtraction computation may be very different than what they do for a multiplication problem. Part of being a good problem solver is figuring out what to check for when solving a particular kind of problem.
3. Pass out Handout 2.4, *Subtracting Fractions.* Ask students to respond to the prompt individually before sharing their ideas with a partner.
4. Spend time talking as a whole class about the student's mistake. Be sure students notice that "Baffled in Boston" is subtracting the smaller fraction from the greater fraction (in each mixed number) without considering the position of the fraction in the context of the expression. This is not correct. We cannot swap fractions, depending on their size. The second mixed number—fraction and whole number—must be subtracted from the first.
5. As you talk about this problem, address strategies for checking the featured student's work and how those strategies can reveal the featured mistake. Students' ideas may include the following:
   a. The student "Baffled in Boston" may want to represent each computation with a model. For example, the student could use a number line to show each subtraction as a take-away problem. (See Figure 2.2.) This may help the student see the errors on the last two problems.

Figure 2.2

b. The student can add the difference to the number that was subtracted to see whether he gets the correct total. (See the following example.)

　　　Check:

$$4\tfrac{1}{8} + 3\tfrac{3}{8} = 7\tfrac{4}{8} \neq 7\tfrac{1}{4}$$

c. The student can think in terms of missing addend and add on in order to find the correct difference (e.g., $3\tfrac{3}{8} + ? = 7\tfrac{1}{4}$).

d. The student may also want to think of a situation for each computation. For example, he can think of a story problem for $7\tfrac{1}{4} - 3\tfrac{3}{8}$ (e.g., *MJ had $7\tfrac{1}{4}$ cups of flour. He used $3\tfrac{3}{8}$ cups for a batch of pancakes. How much flour does he have left?*) Thinking about what to do to solve this problem might help the student realize that $\tfrac{3}{8}$ should be subtracted from $\tfrac{1}{4}$.

6. Following this discussion, ask students to revise and add on to their original responses to incorporate the ideas they talked about during the whole-class discussion.

Extending the Activity

1. Pose the following problem to students:

Imagine a friend wrote, "$8 - 5\tfrac{1}{4} = 3\tfrac{1}{4}$." What mistake did your friend make? What could you say or do to help your friend find the correct difference?

(Possible response: The student computed $8\tfrac{1}{4} - 5$ instead of $8 - 5\tfrac{1}{4}$. I would suggest the friend think of the subtraction as a missing addend addition computation, $5\tfrac{1}{4} + ? = 8$. She can add friendly parts to $5\tfrac{1}{4}$ until she gets to 8; $5\tfrac{1}{4} + \tfrac{3}{4} + 2 = 8$. The answer is the total amount she added on, or $2\tfrac{3}{4}$.)

2. You may want to ask students to post examples of mistakes they have found as a result of checking their work. Encourage students to explain how they found the mistake and what they did to correct it. An example follows.

Mistakes Discovered by Checking Our Work

My original work:

$9\frac{3}{4} + 3\frac{3}{8}$

$9\frac{3}{4} + \frac{1}{4} = 10$

$10 + 3 = 13$

$13 + \frac{2}{8} = 13 + \frac{1}{4} = 13\frac{1}{4}$

How I checked: I checked to see whether $\frac{1}{4} + 3 + \frac{2}{8}$ added up to $3\frac{3}{8}$.
They do not.
Correction:

$9\frac{3}{4} + 3\frac{3}{8}$

$9\frac{3}{4} + \frac{1}{4} = 10$

$10 + 3 = 13$

$13 + \frac{1}{8} = 13\frac{1}{8}$

Activity 2.5 Multiplying Fractions: Comparing the Size of the Product to the Size of the Factors

Handout 2.5 Multiplying Fractions

Read the comic. Then answer the question that follows.

Imagine you were a student in LN's class. How would you respond to the teacher's question?

Overview

Students read a comic strip in which a student has made a faulty overgeneralization about the relationship between the size of the factors and the size of the product. Discussing the mistake provides students with an opportunity to interpret multiplication expressions involving fractions greater than one.

Common Core Connections

Number and Operations—Fractions, 5.B.5A, 5.B.5B

Before You Use This Activity

Before you use this activity, students should have had prior experience interpreting fraction multiplication as repeatedly adding groups of a fraction (e.g., we can think of $3 \times \frac{1}{5}$ as adding 3 groups of $\frac{1}{5}$). Students should also be familiar with thinking about a fraction, $\frac{a}{b}$, as a copies of the unit fraction $\frac{1}{b}$ (e.g., $\frac{3}{5} = 3 \times \frac{1}{5}$).

| **Materials (in Appendix)** | Handout 2.5, *Multiplying Fractions* |

Digging Deeper into the Math

When students study whole-number multiplication, they learn that the product is always greater than the factors. When their work shifts to multiplying fractions by whole numbers, they are surprised that the product may be smaller than the whole number. Some students overgeneralize once again and reason that the product will *always* be less than the whole number, especially if they are taught that fraction multiplication means taking part of the whole number. This overgeneralization creates problems when the fraction in the expression is greater than one. For example, it may not make sense to interpret $\frac{3}{2} \times 21$ as taking a part of 21. To interpret fraction multiplication expressions correctly, students need to consider the size of the fraction to determine whether the product will be greater than or less than the whole-number factor. It is often helpful to think of the improper fraction as a unit fraction scaled up multiple times or to use the scaling interpretation of multiplication to interpret the expression. For example, we can recognize that $\frac{3}{2}$ is equivalent to $1\frac{1}{2}$ and interpret $\frac{3}{2} \times 21$ as $1\frac{1}{2}$ groups of 21. Or we can think of the expression as scaling 21 to make it $1\frac{1}{2}$ times bigger. These interpretations help us determine that the product of $\frac{3}{2} \times 21$ is greater than 21.

Teaching Notes

1. Before you pass out the handout, post the expressions 1×21 and $\frac{3}{2} \times 21$ on the board. Ask students to compare their values.
2. Pass out Handout 2.5, *Multiplying Fractions*. Ask students to read the comic on their own or read it together as a class.
3. Ask students to respond to the writing prompt on their own before turning and talking with a partner about their ideas. When students talk with their partners, listen in on their conversations to help you decide who you might call on during the whole-class discussion. (See Step 4 for important ideas to listen for.)
4. Call the class together for a whole-class discussion.
   a. Begin by discussing possible reasons why LN thinks that 1×21 is greater than $\frac{3}{2} \times 21$. For example, LN might see the fraction $\frac{3}{2}$ and interpret the expression as taking a part of 21.
   b. As a class, generate examples of computations that can be interpreted as taking a part of a whole number. (Possible examples include $\frac{1}{3} \times 21$, $\frac{1}{2} \times 16$, $\frac{3}{4} \times 24$). Ask students whether the product of each expression will be greater than or less than the whole-number factor. Students should note that the product will be less than the whole-number factor because each expression describes taking a part of the whole number.

    c. Contrast these examples with the computation $\frac{3}{2} \times 21$. Ask, "How is this expression different than the ones we just listed?" Students should notice that the fraction in this expression, $\frac{3}{2}$, is greater than 1.

    d. Focus students' attention on the relationship between $\frac{3}{2}$ and the size of the product of $\frac{3}{2} \times 21$. Ask, "Why is it important to notice that $\frac{3}{2}$ is greater than 1? How does that help us compare 1×21 and $\frac{3}{2} \times 21$?" Ask students to turn and talk with a partner before sharing ideas as a whole class. When you talk as a whole class, be sure the discussion includes the following key ideas:

       i. Since $\frac{3}{2}$ is greater than 1, we cannot interpret the expression $\frac{3}{2} \times 21$ as taking a smaller part of 21.

      ii. We can recognize that $\frac{3}{2}$ is equivalent to $1\frac{1}{2}$ and interpret $\frac{3}{2} \times 21$ as $1\frac{1}{2}$ groups of 21 or taking 21 and making it $1\frac{1}{2}$ times bigger. This tells us that the product is greater than 21.

     iii. We can interpret $\frac{3}{2} \times 21$ as $(3 \times \frac{1}{2}) \times 21$. This also helps us see that the product is greater than 21. Since the value of this expression is greater than $(2 \times \frac{1}{2}) \times 21$, it must be greater than 21.

5. Ask students to revise and add on to their original responses to incorporate the ideas from the whole-class discussion.

Extending the Activity

1. Pose the following problem to students:

Imagine a friend says that $\frac{8}{9} \times 18$ has a greater value than $\frac{3}{2} \times 18$ because 8 and 9 are bigger than 3 and 2. What would you say to this friend?

(Possible response: I would encourage my friend to consider the fraction $\frac{8}{9}$ and the fraction $\frac{3}{2}$ instead of the numerators and denominators separately. It is also important to interpret each expression correctly. The expression $\frac{8}{9} \times 18$ can be thought of as $\frac{8}{9}$ of 18, and the expression $\frac{3}{2} \times 18$ can be thought of as $\frac{3}{2}$ of 18. Since $\frac{8}{9} \times 18$ is only part of 18 but $\frac{3}{2} \times 18$ is 18 repeated $1\frac{1}{2}$ times, $\frac{3}{2} \times 18$ is greater in value.)

2. Pose the following problem to students:

Imagine a friend says that $\frac{1}{5} \times 19 \times 2$ has a greater value than $\frac{1}{5} \times 18 \times 4$ because 19 is greater than 18. What would you say to this friend?

(Possible response: I would encourage my friend to think about the commutative property of multiplication and rewrite the expression as follows:

$$\frac{1}{5} \times 19 \times 2 = \frac{1}{5} \times 2 \times 19 = \frac{2}{5} \times 19$$
$$\frac{1}{5} \times 18 \times 4 = \frac{1}{5} \times 4 \times 18 = \frac{4}{5} \times 18$$

This helps us see that the second expression is taking a very big part of 18. Comparing the expressions, we are taking twice as big a part of 18 than 19. Given that 18 and 19 are very close in size, this helps us conclude that the second expression has a greater value.

Activity 2.6 Dividing Fractions: Is $8 \div \frac{1}{2}$ the Same as Finding Half of 8?

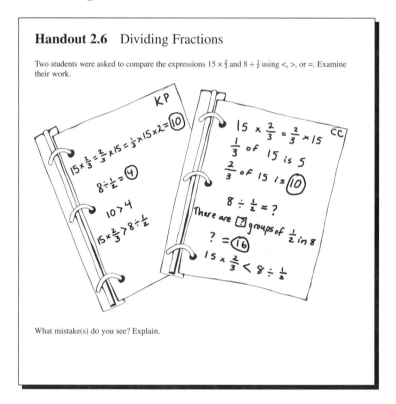

Handout 2.6 Dividing Fractions

Two students were asked to compare the expressions $15 \times \frac{2}{3}$ and $8 \div \frac{1}{2}$ using <, >, or =. Examine their work.

What mistake(s) do you see? Explain.

Overview

In this activity, students examine a common mistake about division of fractions. Students analyze the written work of a student who thinks that $8 \div \frac{1}{2}$ can be interpreted as *half of 8*. By examining and correcting the work, students have the opportunity to discuss how multiplication and division of fractions are different.

Common Core Connections

Number and Operations—Fractions, 5.B.4, 5.B.7

Before You Use This Activity

Before you use this activity in class, students should have had prior experience interpreting division equations in terms of both equal groupings and repeated subtraction. With the first interpretation, we think of an expression such as $12 \div 3$ as "12 divided into 3 groups." With the second, we interpret the expression as the number of groups of 3 that can repeatedly be subtracted from 12.

Materials (in Appendix)   Handout 2.6, *Dividing Fractions*

Digging Deeper into the Math   When students first encounter fraction division, they often misread expressions such as $8 \div \frac{1}{2}$ as *half of 8*. The root of this error may lie in the misconception that division always makes numbers smaller. Students may also make this error because of the words we use to describe sharing. For example, we tend to say *cutting in half* when we talk about sharing items between two people. One way to address this misconception is to emphasize the repeated subtraction interpretation of division when interpreting fraction division expressions. For example, we can read $8 \div \frac{1}{2}$ as repeatedly subtracting groups of one-half from 8. Since there are two halves per whole, there are 2×8, or 16, groups of one-half in 8. Thinking about the action of repeatedly subtracting groups is a powerful way to help students differentiate between $8 \div \frac{1}{2}$ and finding half of 8.

Teaching Notes

1. Pass out Handout 2.6, *Dividing Fractions*. Ask students to examine the student work and respond to the prompt individually before sharing their ideas with a partner.

2. Pull the class together for a whole-class discussion.
   a. Compare the two students' work for $15 \times \frac{2}{3}$. Ask students if they see any mistakes in either student's work. (There aren't any.) Then discuss how the two strategies are similar. Students should note that both students find the product using the commutative property of multiplication. They both use $\frac{1}{3} \times 15$ to calculate $\frac{2}{3} \times 15$.
   b. Ask students to describe the work for $8 \div \frac{1}{2}$. Students should notice that there is a mistake in the second line of KP's work. Specifically, it is not true that $8 \div \frac{1}{2} = 4$. Ask students why KP might have made this mistake. Possible reasons include the following:
      i. The expression $8 \div \frac{1}{2}$ looks like it could be read as *half of 8*.
      ii. Often when we divide, we are making something smaller.
      iii. When we divide, we break something into parts. KP may think that $8 \div \frac{1}{2}$ is the same as breaking something in half or in two parts.

3. After students talk about the reasons KP may interpret $8 \div \frac{1}{2}$ as half of 8, talk about accurate ways to interpret the expression $8 \div \frac{1}{2}$. For example, you could say, "So if $8 \div \frac{1}{2}$ doesn't mean *half of 8*, what does it mean?" Ask students to turn-and-talk with a partner about this question. Listen in on their conversations to identify a student who can interpret this expression as "the number of one-halfs in 8." Ask this student if she will share this idea with the whole class.

4. After talking about $8 \div \frac{1}{2}$ as the number of groups of $\frac{1}{2}$ in 8, ask students to think of an expression that represents half of 8. Students' answers should include $8 \div 2$ and $\frac{1}{2} \times 8$.

5. Because the ideas in this activity are complex, you may wish to scribe key ideas on the board and wrap up the discussion by asking students to compare and contrast the mathematics expressions that arise. (See the following example.)

$8 \div \frac{1}{2}$	$\frac{1}{2} \times 8$	$8 \div 2$
Is <u>not</u> the same as half of 8. Is not the same as $8 \div 2$. Can be interpreted as the number of groups of $\frac{1}{2}$ in 8.	Half of 8.	This is another way to find half of 8.

6. Conclude the discussion by revisiting the sample work. Ask, "How did misinterpreting $8 \div \frac{1}{2}$ as *half of 8* cause KP to answer the question incorrectly? What is the correct comparison between the two expressions?" Students should explain that $8 \div \frac{1}{2} = 16$, which is greater than 10. This tells us that $15 \times \frac{2}{3} < 8 \div \frac{1}{2}$ because $10 < 16$.

7. Give students time to revise their original written work so that it includes the key ideas that surfaced during the whole-class discussion.

Extending the Activity

1. Pose the following problem to students:

    Can $6 \div \frac{1}{3}$ be interpreted as $\frac{1}{3}$ of 6? Why or why not?

    (Possible answer: No, $6 \div \frac{1}{3}$ cannot be interpreted as $\frac{1}{3}$ of 6. We can think of the expression as the number of groups of $\frac{1}{3}$ in 6. When written in symbols, the expression $\frac{1}{3}$ of 6 is written as $\frac{1}{3} \times 6$.)

2. Pose the following problem to students:

    Imagine a friend said that the expressions $\frac{1}{3} \times 12 \frac{3}{8}$ and $12 \frac{3}{8} \div \frac{1}{3}$ have the same value because they both mean find $\frac{1}{3}$ of $12 \frac{3}{8}$. Why might your friend think this? What would you say to your friend to help him or her understand what each expression means?

    (Possible response: The friend might think the two expressions have the same value because we often do think about division when we are finding a part of something. For example, if three people share something, each person gets one-third. But the two expressions are not equivalent. One-third of $12\frac{3}{8}$ is written as $\frac{1}{3} \times 12\frac{3}{8}$. The expression $12\frac{3}{8} \div \frac{1}{3}$ is read as the number of groups of $\frac{1}{3}$ in $12\frac{3}{8}$; it does not represent $\frac{1}{3}$ of $12\frac{3}{8}$.)

3. Post the number line (see Figure 2.3) and pose the following problem to students:

The posted number line could be used to model the expression $\frac{1}{4} \times 2$. Imagine a friend said, "Can't it also be used to model $2 \div \frac{1}{4}$?" Why might your friend ask this? How would you respond to your friend?"

Figure 2.3

(Possible response: The number line models $\frac{1}{4} \times 2$ because it shows one-fourth of the distance between 0 and 2. No, it cannot also be used to model $2 \div \frac{1}{4}$. The expression $2 \div \frac{1}{4}$ does not mean $\frac{1}{4}$ of 2. It can be interpreted as the number of groups of $\frac{1}{4}$ in 2. A number line model for $2 \div \frac{1}{4}$ could look like the one that follows; see Figure 2.4.)

Figure 2.4

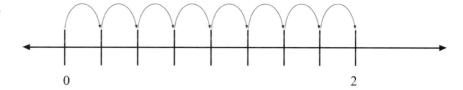

Chapter 3

Decimals

Students' work with decimals in grades four and five requires them to connect and extend ideas about both fractions and whole numbers. For example, students must learn how to write and recognize common fractions as decimals and compare rational numbers in different forms. Students must also learn how to extend ideas about the base ten place value system to perform computational procedures with decimal numbers. Typical mistakes include overgeneralizing ideas about fractions to decimal numbers and applying procedures without connecting them to their underlying concepts. Addressing these common errors can help students develop a robust understanding of the sets of whole and rational numbers and the relationships between them.

Activity 3.1   Connecting Fractions and Decimals: Why Isn't $\frac{1}{5}$ = 0.15?

Activity 3.2   Decimals and Place Value: Is it 20 Tenths or 20 Hundredths?

Activity 3.3   Comparing Decimals: Does Longer Always Mean Larger?

Activity 3.4   Subtracting Decimals: Using Distance to Find Difference

Activity 3.5   Dividing Decimals: Do I Double or Halve?

Activity 3.1   Connecting Fractions and Decimals: Why Isn't $\frac{1}{5}$ = 0.15?

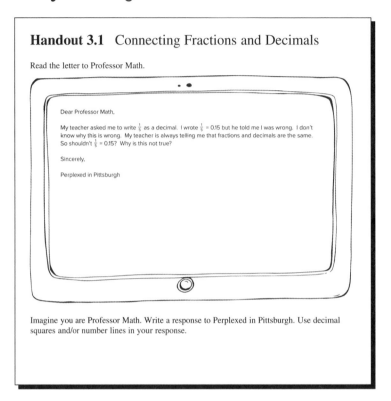

Handout 3.1   Connecting Fractions and Decimals

Read the letter to Professor Math.

Dear Professor Math,

My teacher asked me to write $\frac{1}{5}$ as a decimal. I wrote $\frac{1}{5}$ = 0.15 but he told me I was wrong. I don't know why this is wrong. My teacher is always telling me that fractions and decimals are the same. So shouldn't $\frac{1}{5}$ = 0.15? Why is this not true?

Sincerely,

Perplexed in Pittsburgh

Imagine you are Professor Math. Write a response to Perplexed in Pittsburgh. Use decimal squares and/or number lines in your response.

Overview

This activity focuses on a misconception that frequently occurs when students are asked to write fractions using decimal notation. Students read a letter to Professor Math from a student who thinks that $\frac{1}{5}$ = 0.15. Discussing the mistake provides students with an opportunity to think carefully about the idea of equivalence and what we mean when we say that two numbers are the same.

Common Core Connections

Number and Operations—Fractions, 4.C.6

Before You Use This Activity

Before you use this activity, students should have had prior experience representing decimal numbers to hundredths using decimal squares and number lines. Students should also have had the opportunity to use these tools to represent common fractions (e.g., $\frac{1}{2}$, $\frac{1}{4}$, and $\frac{3}{4}$) using decimal notation. Several examples are given in Figures 3.1, 3.2, and 3.3.

Figure 3.1 $\frac{1}{2} = 0.5$

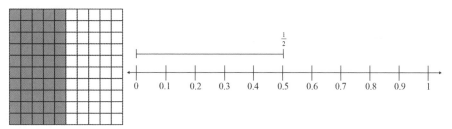

Figure 3.2 $\frac{1}{4} = 0.25$

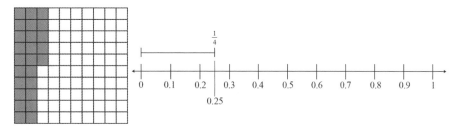

Figure 3.3 $\frac{3}{4} = 0.75$

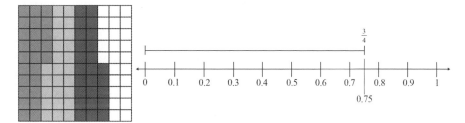

Materials (in Appendix)   Handout 3.1, *Connecting Fractions and Decimals*
Decimal Squares
Decimal Number Lines

Digging Deeper into the Math   This activity focuses on the idea of equivalence and uses decimal squares and number lines to help students understand what it means when a particular fraction and decimal are the same. When students work with equivalent forms of rational numbers, they may be tempted to focus on the surface features of the numerals. For example, if they are asked to write $\frac{1}{5}$ as a decimal, students may write 0.15, thinking that the digits 1 and 5 must appear in the decimal form of the number. Students must move beyond this superficial (and flawed) understanding of equivalence and learn that a fraction and decimal are the same, or equivalent, if they both represent the same value. Decimal squares and number lines are very effective models for proving or disproving an equivalent relationship between a fraction and a decimal. For example, the fraction $\frac{1}{5}$ is written as the decimal number 0.2 because both numerals represent the same shaded region of a decimal square and the same location on the number line. (See Figure 3.4.)

Figure 3.4 $\frac{1}{5} = 0.2 = 0.20$

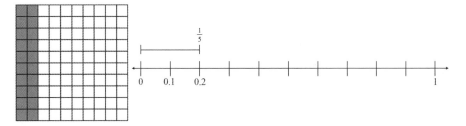

Teaching Notes

1. Begin this activity by asking students to show the fraction $\frac{1}{5}$ on a decimal square and number line. (Decimal squares and decimal number lines are provided in the Appendix.)

2. Pass out Handout 3.1, *Connecting Fractions and Decimals.* Ask students to write their responses on their own before sharing their ideas with a partner. As students talk, listen in on their conversations and use this information to help you decide who to call on during the whole-class discussion. (See Step 3 for ideas to listen for.)

3. Call the class together for a whole-class discussion.

    a. First, focus the discussion on the similarities between fractions and decimals. You might ask, "The writer writes, *My teacher is always telling me that fractions and decimals are the same.* What do you think she means by that?" Students may note that fractions and decimals have a lot in common. For example, both fractions and decimals represent parts of wholes. When we talk about equal parts, we can name those parts with fractions or decimals.

    b. Ask students to talk about how fractions and decimals are different. Students may note that fractions can show equal parts that are any size, but decimals can only show equal parts made up of tenths, hundredths, thousandths, and so forth.

    c. Ask students to use a decimal square and number line to explain what it means for a fraction and a decimal to be equivalent. You might say, "We write that $\frac{1}{2} = 0.5$, and we say that the two numbers are equivalent. But what exactly does that mean? Can you explain using a decimal square or number line?" Students should note that the fraction $\frac{1}{2}$ and the decimal 0.5 are equivalent because they represent the same value. We can use either $\frac{1}{2}$ or 0.5 to show the same amount of shading on a decimal grid or mark the same location on the number line.

    d. Next, talk about why the writer might think that $\frac{1}{5}$ is equivalent to 0.15 when written as a decimal. Students will likely note that because the fraction $\frac{1}{5}$ has a 1 and 5 in it, it seems reasonable that its decimal form will, too. Students may also note that many fractions look very similar to their decimal equivalences. For example, $\frac{2}{10} = 0.2$, $\frac{3}{100} = 0.03$, and $\frac{23}{100} = 0.23$. So, it is understandable why the student might think that all fraction and decimal equivalences should look alike. (*Note*: Any fraction whose numerator is a whole number and whose denominator is a power of 10 will have a decimal value with the same digits as its numerator.)

e. Ask for volunteers to show why $\frac{1}{5} \neq 0.15$ using a decimal square. Be sure that the discussion focuses on the following key ideas:

Figure 3.5

$\frac{1}{5} = 0.2 = 0.20$ \qquad 0.15

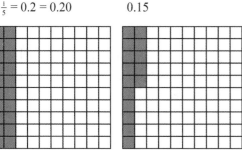

    i. If $\frac{1}{5}$ is equivalent to 0.15, both numbers must represent the same amount of shading on the decimal square. But they don't. The fraction $\frac{1}{5}$ can be thought of as 1 out of 5 parts. If we divide the square into five parts, one part is two-tenths (0.2) or twenty-hundredths (0.20). This is not the same as 0.15. So, $\frac{1}{5} \neq 0.15$. (See Figure 3.5.)

    a. Ask for volunteers to show why $\frac{1}{5} \neq 0.15$ using a number line. Be sure that the discussion focuses on the following key ideas:

    ii. If $\frac{1}{5} = 0.15$, then both numbers would mark the same location on a number line. But this is not true. The fraction $\frac{1}{5}$ can be thought of as 1 out of 5 parts. If we divide the distance between 0 and 1 into 5 parts, the fraction $\frac{1}{5}$ can be used to mark the location of the number that is $\frac{1}{5}$ of the way between 0 and 1. To find the decimal form of $\frac{1}{5}$, we can divide each fifth into two equal parts. This creates ten parts. The decimal 0.2 marks the same distance as the fraction $\frac{1}{5}$. The decimal 0.15 can be thought of as one-tenth and five-hundredths (i.e., $0.15 = 0.1 + 0.05$). If we move one-tenth and five-hundredths (or half of another tenth) to the right of zero, we are at a different location than $\frac{1}{5}$. So, $\frac{1}{5} \neq 0.15$. (See Figure 3.6.)

Figure 3.6

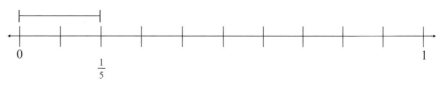

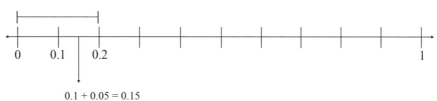

4. Wrap up the activity by asking students to revise their written responses so that they can include ideas from the whole-class discussion.

1. Ask students the following question:

    Imagine a friend thinks that $\frac{3}{4}$ is written as 0.34 when written as a decimal. Why might your friend think this? How can you use a number line or decimal square to help your friend find and fix this error?

    (Possible answer: The friend might think that 0.34 is equivalent to $\frac{3}{4}$ because they both have the same digits. The friend might think that, when a fraction is rewritten as a decimal, the same digits must appear in both. This is not true. The friend can find the error by shading $\frac{3}{4}$ on one decimal square and 0.34 on another and noticing that the shaded areas are not equal. The friend can correct the error using the equivalent relationship between $\frac{1}{4}$ and 0.25. Since $\frac{3}{4} = \frac{1}{4} + \frac{1}{4} + \frac{1}{4}$, we know that $\frac{3}{4} = 0.25 + 0.25 + 0.25 = 0.75$.)

2. Pose the following question to students:

    Examine the following multiple-choice question:
    Which number is equivalent to 5.4?
       A. $\frac{5}{4}$
       B. 5.04
       C. 54.0
       D. $5\frac{2}{5}$

    Imagine a student, RL, chose letter A. Why might RL have made this choice? What would you say to RL to help her find and correct this mistake?

    (Possible answer: The student might think the two are equivalent because they both have the same digits. This answer is not correct, however, because $\frac{5}{4} = 1\frac{1}{4}$ and that is not equivalent to 5.4. If RL reads the decimal, 5.4, as five and four-tenths and thinks about the equivalent relationship between tenths and fifths, she can determine that the correct answer is D; $5.4 = 5\frac{4}{10} = 5\frac{2}{5}$.)

Activity 3.2 Decimals and Place Value: Is It 20 Tenths or 20 Hundredths?

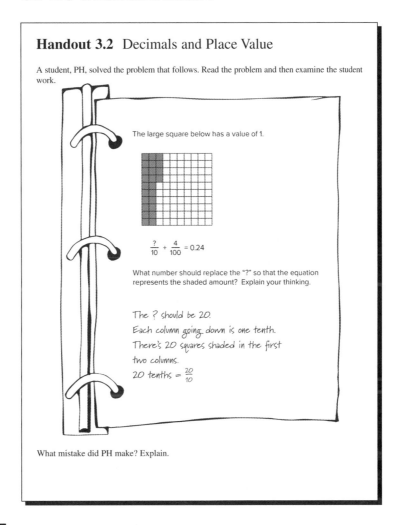

Handout 3.2 Decimals and Place Value

A student, PH, solved the problem that follows. Read the problem and then examine the student work.

The large square below has a value of 1.

$\frac{?}{10} + \frac{4}{100} = 0.24$

What number should replace the "?" so that the equation represents the shaded amount? Explain your thinking.

The ? should be 20.
Each column going down is one tenth.
There's 20 squares shaded in the first two columns.
20 tenths = $\frac{20}{10}$

What mistake did PH make? Explain.

Overview

This activity focuses on the relationship between tenths and hundredths. The featured task focuses on expressing a decimal number as the sum of two fractions whose denominators are 10 and 100. The student work shows that the student has confused 20 tenths with 20 hundredths. By discussing the mistake, students have the opportunity to think deeply about the relationship between tenths and hundredths as they are written using both fraction and decimal notation.

Common Core Connections

Number and Operations–Fractions, 4.C.5, 4.C.6; Number and Operations in Base Ten, 5.A.1, 5.A.3, 5.A.3.A

Before You Use This Activity

Before you use this activity in class, students should have had prior experiences representing decimal numbers to tenths and hundredths using decimal squares.

Materials (in Appendix) Handout 3.2, *Decimals and Place Value*
Decimal Squares
Decimal Number Lines

Digging Deeper into the Math   Tools such as decimal squares offer tremendous potential to help students make sense of key ideas related to decimals. When teachers use decimal squares in class, however, they must remember that the ideas the decimal squares are intended to illuminate are not immediately obvious to students.

Figure 3.7

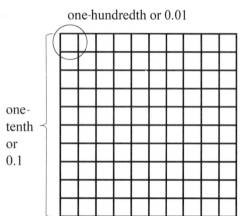

one-hundredth or 0.01

one-tenth or 0.1

Instead, students must work with the decimal squares and talk about their ideas so that they form meaningful and accurate connections between these tools and the characteristics of decimal numbers. When students use decimal squares to explore decimal numbers to hundredths, their work should help them develop understanding of the following key ideas: If the entire square represents the whole, (a) each column (or row) represents one-tenth, or 0.1, of the square; (b) each smaller square represents one-hundredth, or 0.01, of the square; (c) each hundredth is ten times smaller than each tenth; and, as a result, (d) ten-hundredths are equivalent to one-tenth (i.e., 0.10 = 0.1 or $\frac{10}{100} = \frac{1}{10}$). (See Figure 3.7.)

Teaching Notes

1. Post the task embedded in this activity on the board. Ask students to answer the same question that the (fictitious) student, PH, answered incorrectly (i.e., "What number should replace the '?' so that the equation represents the shaded amount? Explain your thinking.")

2. Pass out Handout 3.2, *Decimals and Place Value*, and ask students to respond silently on their own before sharing their ideas with a partner. When students talk with a partner, listen in on their conversations, and use that information to identify possible speakers for whole-class discussion. (See Step 3 for ideas on what to listen for.)

3. Call the class back together for a whole-class discussion.
   a. Ask students to generate possible reasons PH might think the missing number is 20. Students may respond that PH likely notices that there are two full columns shaded. Inside those two columns are 20 small squares. Since each column is one-tenth, he might think that the 20 squares represent 20 tenths of the area.
   b. Ask students what is wrong with PH's reasoning. Students should respond that the missing number should tell how many tenths are shaded. Since each column represents one-tenth, the missing number should be 2. Although it is true that 20 squares are shaded in those columns, the squares represent hundredths: $\frac{20}{100} = \frac{2}{10}$.
   c. To help students think deeply about the relationship between tenths and hundredths, say the following: "Okay, so we agree that the

number 2 should replace the question mark to get $\frac{2}{10} + \frac{4}{100} = 0.24$. But when I look at that equation, that seems strange to me. How could it be that 2 plus 4 [pointing to the two numerators] equals 24? How does that make sense?" Students should note that 2 and 4 have different denominators and that the 2 represents 2 tenths. If we want to add $\frac{2}{10}$ to $\frac{4}{100}$, we need to think of $\frac{2}{10}$ as 20 hundredths; $\frac{2}{10} + \frac{4}{100} = \frac{20}{100} + \frac{4}{100} = 0.24$.

4. Focus students' attention on the relationship between tenths and hundredths. Post the following statements on the board and ask students to use the decimal square to show why the first two show equivalent relationships but the last one does not.

$\frac{2}{10} = \frac{20}{100}$

$0.2 = 0.20$

$\frac{20}{10} \neq \frac{20}{100}$

Be sure that the discussion stays focused on the relationship between tenths and hundredths. For example, by looking at the decimal square, students can see that since hundredths are ten times smaller than tenths, it takes ten times as many hundredths to cover the same area as two-tenths. Be sure to also address the meaning of the number "20 tenths" so that students don't assume it's just a nonsense number. Students can reason that since 10 tenths is one whole, 20 tenths is equivalent to two wholes.

5. Wrap up the activity by asking students to revise their written responses so that they can include ideas from the whole-class discussion.

Extending the Activity

1. Post the decimal square (see Figure 3.8) and pose the following task to students:

Imagine a friend wrote the following number sentence for the shaded part of this decimal square: $\frac{30}{10} + \frac{5}{100} = 0.35$. What error did your friend make? How might you help your friend fix this error?

(Possible answer: The student has written the fraction $\frac{30}{10}$ to represent the three shaded columns. This is not correct. Each column represents $\frac{1}{10}$ of the square so three columns is $\frac{3}{10}$, not $\frac{30}{10}$. The correct equation is $\frac{3}{10} + \frac{5}{100} = 0.35$.)

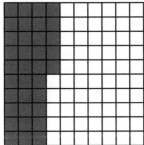
Figure 3.8

2. Post the number line (see Figure 3.9) and pose the following task to students:

Imagine a friend used the number sentence $\frac{20}{10} + \frac{3}{10} = 0.23$ to represent the location of 0.23 on a number line.

Figure 3.9

What errors did your friend make? How might you help your friend fix these errors?

(Possible answer: The friend made two errors. First, the friend wrote $\frac{20}{10}$ instead of $\frac{2}{10}$. One way to fix the error is to think of the number 0.2 as two times one-tenth, or $\frac{2}{10}$. Second, the friend wrote $\frac{3}{10}$ instead of $\frac{3}{100}$. The friend can fix the error by remembering that even though the distance between 0.2 and 0.3 is split into ten intervals, each interval is $\frac{1}{100}$ because 100 of these intervals make up one unit. The correct equation is $\frac{2}{10} + \frac{3}{100} = 0.23$.)

Activity 3.3   Comparing Decimals: Does Longer Always Mean Larger?

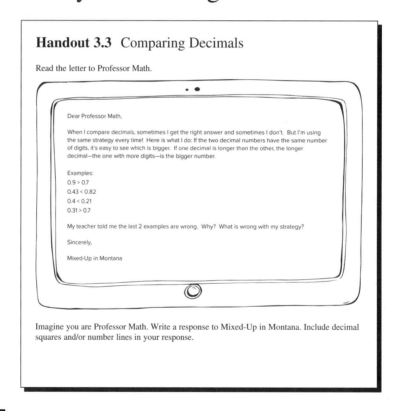

Handout 3.3 Comparing Decimals

Read the letter to Professor Math.

Dear Professor Math,

When I compare decimals, sometimes I get the right answer and sometimes I don't. But I'm using the same strategy every time! Here is what I do: If the two decimal numbers have the same number of digits, it's easy to see which is bigger. If one decimal is longer than the other, the longer decimal—the one with more digits—is the bigger number.

Examples:
0.9 > 0.7
0.43 < 0.82
0.4 < 0.21
0.31 > 0.7

My teacher told me the last 2 examples are wrong. Why? What is wrong with my strategy?

Sincerely,

Mixed-Up in Montana

Imagine you are Professor Math. Write a response to Mixed-Up in Montana. Include decimal squares and/or number lines in your response.

Overview

This activity features the common mistake of comparing decimals according to their lengths without looking more closely at the values of the digits. The letter to Professor Math focuses on a student who reasons that 0.4 < 0.21 because 0.21 is longer than 0.4. In this activity, students unravel the misconception that *longer means larger* and form more reliable strategies for comparing decimal numbers.

Common Core Connections

Number and Operations—Fractions, 4.C.7; Number and Operations in Base Ten, 5.A.3, 5.A.3.B

Before you Use This Activity

Before you use this activity in class, students should have had prior experiences representing decimal numbers to hundredths using decimal squares and number lines. Students should have also had experiences using these representations to explore the relationships between tenths and hundredths (e.g., $\frac{1}{10} = \frac{10}{100}$, $0.1 = 0.10$, $\frac{1}{100}$ is ten times smaller than $\frac{1}{10}$).

Materials (in Appendix)

Handout 3.3, *Comparing Decimals*
Decimal Squares
Decimal Number Lines

Digging Deeper into the Math

When students compare two decimal numbers, they often think longer means larger. That is, they reason that the decimal with the greater number of digits always has the greater value. This misconception is rooted in students' work with whole numbers. If given two whole numbers such that one has more digits than the other, the number with the greater number of digits will always be greater than the other number. Students may be particularly reluctant to abandon the overgeneralization because it sometimes yields correct results (e.g., 0.81 > 0.7). As a general rule, however, it is not true that longer means larger when comparing decimal numbers. This is because each place in our number system is one-tenth, or ten times, smaller than the place to the left. As decimal numbers grow in length, each additional digit has a value that is ten times smaller than the digit to its left. When comparing two decimals to the hundredths, we need to consider both the face value and place value of the digits before we can determine which is greater. For example, 0.81 is greater than 0.7 because 0.81 has more tenths than 0.7, not because 0.81 is longer than 0.7. By contrast, 0.4 is greater than 0.37, even though 0.37 is longer or has more digits, because 0.4 has more tenths than 0.37.

Teaching Notes

1. Launch this activity by asking students to find the greater decimal in each pair below. Pass out decimal squares to help students form accurate comparisons.
   0.9 ? 0.7
   0.43 ? 0.82
   0.4 ? 0.21
   0.31 ? 0.7
2. Pass out Handout 3.3, *Comparing Decimals,* and ask students to write their responses individually before sharing ideas with their partners.
3. Call the class back together for a whole-class discussion.

a. Talk first about why the writer might think that decimals with more digits are always greater than decimals with fewer digits. Where might this idea come from? Students should note that this idea is true for whole numbers. If one whole number has more digits than another, it will always be greater than the other number. Once this idea comes up, talk about why this is true. Students should focus on the fact that each place value in our number system is larger than the one to its right. That is why whole numbers grow in size as they grow in length (i.e., number of digits).

b. Next, talk about why this idea is not true for decimals. You might say, "If a whole number with more digits is always greater than a whole number with fewer digits, why isn't this true for decimal numbers? For example, why isn't a decimal with two digits always greater than a decimal with one digit?" While students may quickly agree that the generalization does not hold for decimals, explaining why it doesn't hold true is likely to be much more difficult. You may want to ask students to think quietly for twenty to thirty seconds before sharing their ideas with a partner. When you call the class back together, be sure the following key ideas surface in the discussion.

i. If a decimal has more digits than another, it may not be greater than a decimal with fewer digits. This is because place values grow smaller as we move to the right; each place value is ten times smaller than the place to the left. Hundredths, for example, are ten times smaller than tenths. We can see this relationship on a decimal grid or number line. (See Figure 3.10.)

Figure 3.10

ii. If a decimal number is made up of tenths and hundredths, we don't know whether it is less than or greater than a number made up of only tenths until we look at the value of the digits. If the longer decimal has fewer tenths than the other, it is smaller. This is true even if it has some additional hundredths because hundredths are smaller than tenths.

iii. Decomposing decimals into tenths and hundredths may also help us see why longer decimals are not always greater than shorter ones. For example, if we want to compare 0.7 and 0.31, we can rewrite 0.31 as 0.3 + 0.01. We can see that 0.31 has only three tenths while 0.7 is made up of seven tenths. So, 0.31 is smaller. We really don't even need to consider that 0.31 has an additional hundredth because hundredths are smaller pieces than tenths. (See Figure 3.11.)

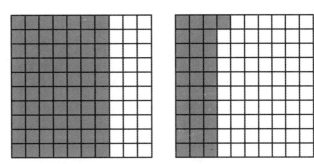

Figure 3.11

    iv. Rewriting a decimal number in an equivalent form can help us compare decimals accurately. For example, we can rewrite 0.7 as 0.70 and conclude that 0.70 > 0.31 (i.e., 70-hundredths is greater than 31-hundredths.)

4. Wrap up the discussion by asking students to revisit the writer's original error. You might say, "Let's suppose that Mixed-Up in Montana listened to our discussion and said, 'Okay, but my strategy does work sometimes. For example, 0.81 > 0.7 and 0.81 is longer than 0.7. Why does my strategy work here?'" Students should respond that the reason 0.81 is greater than 0.7 is because it has more tenths, not because it has more digits.

5. Wrap up the activity by asking students to revise their written responses so that they can include ideas from the whole-class discussion.

Extending the Activity

1. Pose the following question to students:

Imagine a friend thinks 0.4 < 0.40 because 40 is ten times greater than 4. Use a decimal square or number line to help your friend find and fix this error.

(Possible answer: I would show each number, 0.4 and 0.40, on a decimal grid so that the friend could see that both numbers are equal since they represent the same area.) (See Figure 3.12.)

Figure 3.12

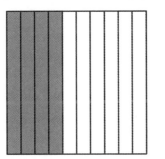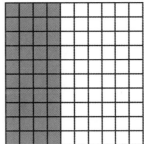

2. Pose the following task to students:

Imagine a friend was given the following task: One digit is missing from the comparison 0.4? □ 0.31. Do you still have enough information to determine the greater decimal in each pair? Why or why not?

Imagine the friend said, "No, we do not have enough information because we can't see the hundredths digit of the first number. If that digit is greater than one, the number could be greater than 0.31." How would you respond to this friend?

(Possible answer: I would encourage my friend to read the first number, 0.4?, as four-tenths plus some number of hundredths and the second number, 0.31, as three-tenths plus one-hundredth. Since the first number has more tenths than the second, we can conclude that it is greater than 0.31 even without knowing the value of its hundredths digit. *Note*: If you are working with students in grades five or higher, you can modify this activity to include numbers in the thousandths.)

Activity 3.4   Subtracting Decimals: Using Distance to Find Difference

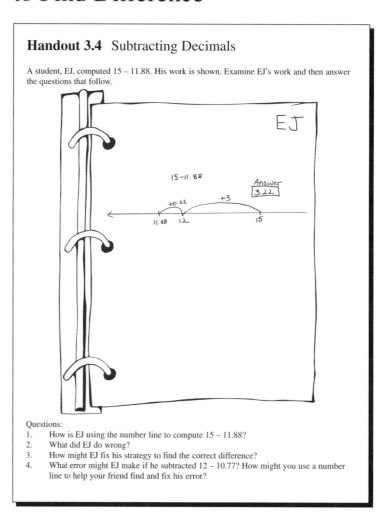

Handout 3.4 Subtracting Decimals

A student, EJ, computed 15 – 11.88. His work is shown. Examine EJ's work and then answer the questions that follow.

Questions:
1. How is EJ using the number line to compute 15 – 11.88?
2. What did EJ do wrong?
3. How might EJ fix his strategy to find the correct difference?
4. What error might EJ make if he subtracted 12 – 10.77? How might you use a number line to help your friend find and fix his error?

Overview

In this activity, students examine a strategy for subtracting 15 – 11.88. The mistake embedded in the strategy provides students with an opportunity to talk about the *distance* interpretation of subtraction, the use of an open number line as a tool for subtracting decimals, and the relationship between tenths and hundredths.

Common Core Connections

Number and Operations in Base Ten, 5.B.7

Before You Use This Activity

Before using this activity, be sure your students have had prior experiences thinking about decimal subtraction in terms of missing addend or distance. For example, we can compute 4 – 3.2 by asking, "3.2 plus *what* equals 4?," or 3.2 + ? = 4. We can represent this computation on a number line in terms of the distance between 3.2 and 4. (See Figure 3.13.)

Figure 3.13

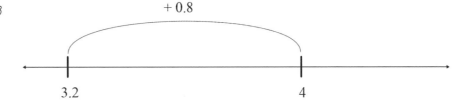

If students are unfamiliar with subtracting on the open number line, you may want to try a few examples with whole numbers. (See Figure 3.14.)

Figure 3.14   112 - 74 = ?

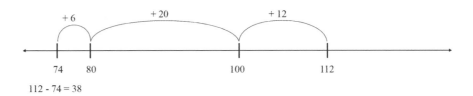

112 - 74 = 38

208 - 143 = ?

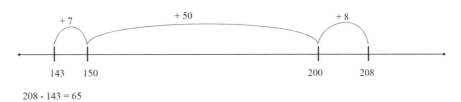

208 - 143 = 65

Materials (in Appendix)

Handout 3.4, *Subtracting Decimals*
Decimal Squares

Digging Deeper into the Math A computation such as 15 − 11.88 can be interpreted as the distance between 11.88 and 15 on a number line. That is, we can find the difference by determining the *distance* from 11.88 to 15. Since this number is not immediately obvious, we can find it by making smaller and friendlier jumps from 11.88 until we get to 15. Since whole numbers are typically friendlier numbers than decimals, we may want to add on to 11.88 so that we land on 12, the nearest whole number. For example, we can add 11.88 + 0.02 = 11.9; 11.9 + 0.1 = 12. (See Figure 3.15.)

Figure 3.15

We can add 12 + 3 to get 15 and then find the total length of all the jumps to determine 15 − 11.88 = 3.12. (See Figure 3.16.)

Figure 3.16

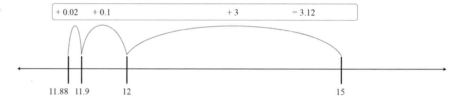

Finding difference in terms of distance is an effective and accessible strategy for students because they can modify the size of the jumps in different ways. However, students must think carefully about place value and partial sums as they make their jumps. For example, the featured mistake in this activity shows the work of a student who reasons that 11.88 + 0.22 = 12. Identifying common errors and talking about distances on a number line can help students think deeply about the relationships between whole numbers, tenths, and hundredths. (*Note*: The number lines featured in this activity are typically called *open*, or *empty*, number lines. This type of number line has no markers or tick marks and does not require that locations be proportionally accurate—e.g., a distance of 0.1 should be longer than a distance of 0.01 but need not be ten times as long.)

Teaching Notes

1. Post the computation 15 − 11.88 on the board. Ask the students to find the difference in two different ways.
2. Pass out Handout 3.4, *Subtracting Decimals,* and ask students to read and respond to Questions 1–3 on their own before talking with a partner.

   As students talk with a partner, listen in on their conversations to help you decide who you might call on during the whole-class discussion. (See Step 3 for important ideas to listen for.) Ask these students to talk about these ideas later during the whole-class discussion.

3. Call the class together for a whole-class discussion.

   a. Focus the discussion first on how EJ interprets the computation 15 – 11.88. Students must understand that EJ is interpreting the subtraction as the distance between 11.88 and 15 on the number line.

   b. Next, focus on EJ's mistake. Be sure students can explain why 0.88 + 0.22 ≠ 1. One way to see why 0.88 + 0.22 ≠ 1 is to break each number into tenths and hundredths and then use the commutative property of addition:

      0.88 + 0.22 = 0.8 + 0.08 + 0.2 + 0.02 = 0.8 + 0.2 + 0.08 + 0.02 = 1.0 + 0.1 = 1.1

   c. Third, talk about alternate ways that EJ can use his strategy correctly.

      i. Launch this part of the discussion by asking why it makes sense to add on to 11.88 to get to 12. Students should note that 12 is a friendly number because it is a whole number. If we can find the distance from 11.88 to 12, finding the rest of the distance to 15 will be easy.

      ii. Ask students what EJ can do to get from 11.88 to 12. For example, students may explain that EJ can add 0.02 to get to 11.9 and then 0.1 to get to 12. Show this on the number line. (See Figure 3.15.)

      iii. Be sure students can use the number line representation to find the answer to the computation. You might ask, "Once EJ gets to 15, now what? How does he use his work to find the answer to 15 – 11.88?" Students should note that the answer is the total distance between the two numbers. This is calculated by adding the distance of all the jumps EJ took to get from 11.88 to 15. (See Figure 3.16.)

4. Wrap up the activity by asking students to answer Discussion Question 4 from the handout. If students answered this question at the start of the activity, ask them to revisit the question using the information gleaned in the whole-class discussion.

Extending the Activity

1. Post the number line (see Figure 3.17) and pose the following prompt:

   Imagine a friend tried to compute 16.2 – 12.1 as shown. What error(s) did your friend make? What is the correct difference?

Figure 3.17

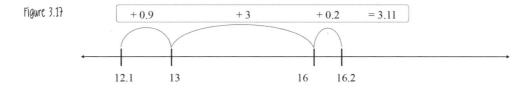

(Possible answer: The friend added 0.9 and 0.2 to get 0.11. This is not correct; $0.9 + 0.2 = 0.9 + 0.1 + 0.1 = 1.1$. The correct difference is $3 + 1.1$ or 4.1.)

2. Post the number lines (see Figure 3.18) and pose the following prompt:

    Imagine two students tried to compute 11.34 – 9.77 by finding the distance from 9.77 to 11.34. What do you think of each student's steps so far? How are they similar? How are they different? What might each do next?

Figure 3.18

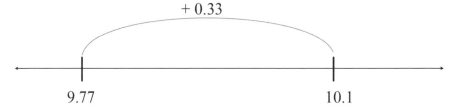

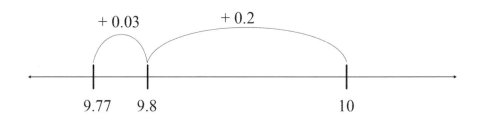

(Possible response: Both students rely on friendly numbers to find the distance in smaller, friendlier parts. The students' work differs in how they break up the total distance into smaller parts. The first student adds 0.33 to land on the number 10.1. This student could then add 0.9 to get to 11 and then 0.34 to get to 11.34. The second student adds 0.03 to land on the number 9.8. Then this student adds 0.2 to land on the whole number 10. This student can now add 1 to get to 11 and then 0.34 to get to 11.34. Both students should add the total distance jumped to find the difference.)

Activity 3.5 Dividing Decimals: Do I Double or Halve?

Handout 3.5 Dividing Decimals

Read the comic. Then answer the questions that follow.

Questions:
1. Which strategy do you think gives the correct quotient of 7 ÷ 0.2? Why?
2. What is the other student's mistake?
3. How do you think each student, MJ and LL, might compute 8 ÷ 0.4? Which strategy gives the correct quotient?

Overview

The comic strip featured in this activity focuses on the division 7 ÷ 0.2. In the comic strip, two students offer different and opposing computational strategies. Discussing the two strategies—and finding the one that works—gives students the opportunity to think about how to use the quotient of 7 ÷ 0.1 to derive the quotient of 7 ÷ 0.2.

Common Core Connections

Number and Operations in Base Ten, 5.B.7

Before You Use This Activity

Be sure students have had prior experiences with decimal computations that involve division by one-tenth. Students should also be familiar with the repeated subtraction or measurement interpretation of division in which the dividend represents a total and the divisor represents the size of each group.

For example, when interpreting $7 \div 0.1$ in terms of repeated subtraction, we read the expression as *the number of groups of one-tenth in seven.*

Materials (in Appendix)

Handout 3.5, *Dividing Decimals*
Decimal Squares (optional)
Decimal Number Lines (optional)

Digging Deeper into the Math

The mistake in this activity focuses on computing $7 \div 0.2$ using the related division $7 \div 0.1$. The computation $7 \div 0.1$ is easy to perform if one thinks in terms of the repeated subtraction interpretation of division. Dividing a number by 0.1 can be interpreted as repeatedly subtracting groups of one-tenth; there are 10 one-tenths per whole. (See Figure 3.19.)

Figur 3.19

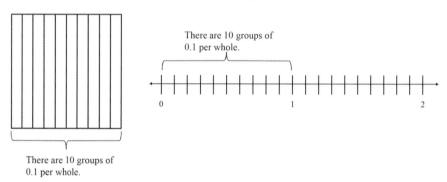

There are 10 groups of
0.1 per whole.

There are 10 groups of
0.1 per whole.

With this interpretation, we read the expression $7 \div 0.1$ as the number of groups of one-tenth in 7. Since there are 10 one-tenths per whole and there are 7 wholes, we can reason that $7 \div 0.1 = 70$. We can use the quotient of $7 \div 0.1$ to find the quotient of $7 \div 0.2$, which we read as the number of groups of two-tenths in 7. Since the groups are twice as big, the total number of groups is cut in half. In other words, since there are now two-tenths in each group, there are half as many groups. This tells us that the quotient of $7 \div 0.2$ is *half* the quotient of $7 \div 0.1$, or 35.

Teaching Notes

1. Post the computation $7 \div 0.2 = ?$ on the board and ask students to find the quotient using two different strategies.
2. Pass out Handout 3.5, *Dividing Decimals,* and ask students to read and respond on their own before sharing their ideas with a partner.
3. Conduct a whole-class discussion of students' ideas. Focus the discussion on the following key ideas:
   a. Spend some time making sure students understand how MJ is interpreting the expression $7 \div 0.1$ and how he is using that interpretation to reason that $7 \div 0.1 = 70$. Have decimal squares and/or decimal number lines ready for students to use to show their thinking.

b. Ask why it may help MJ to use 7 ÷ 0.1 to find 7 ÷ 0.2. Students may respond that it is easy to count the number of groups of one-tenth per whole and then multiply that by 7. (See figures in the section, "Digging Deeper into the Math.")

c. Ask students to identify the strategy that yields the correct quotient. Students should respond that LL's strategy is correct. The expression 7 ÷ 0.2 can be thought of as the number of groups of two-tenths in 7. Groups of two-tenths are twice the size of groups of one-tenth. Since the size of each group has doubled, the number of groups is cut in half. We know there are 70 groups of one-tenth in 7, so there are half as many (or 35) groups of two-tenths in 7. LL is correct; we should divide 70 by 2 to get the final quotient of 35.

d. Focus on the flaw in MJ's strategy. You might say, "Why might MJ have thought it made sense to multiply 70 by 2? Why is that wrong?" Students may respond that MJ multiplies 70 by 2 because 0.2 is two times 0.1 (or 0.1 × 2 = 0.2). This strategy is not correct, however, because 7 ÷ 0.1 = 70; there are 70 groups of 0.1 in 70. If we want groups of two-tenths, we can make only 35, not 140.

4. Wrap up the activity by asking students to answer Discussion Question 3 from the handout. If students answered this question at the start of the activity, ask them to revisit the question using the information gleaned in the whole-class discussion.

Extending the Activity

1. Pose the following problem to students:

   GG used 12 ÷ 0.1 to find the quotient of 12 ÷ 0.3. Here is GG's work:

   > *12 ÷ 0.3 = ?*
   > *12 ÷ 0.1 = 120*
   > *120 × 3 = 360*
   > *12 ÷ 0.3 = 360*

   Did GG get the correct answer? Why or why not?

   (Possible response: GG did not get the correct answer. Because 0.3 is three times 0.1, GG should compute 120 ÷ 3 = 40 to find the quotient. When we divide, if we triple the size of the groups, the number of groups is reduced by a factor of 3.)

2. Pose the following problem to students:

   RT used the quotient of 12 ÷ 3 to find the quotient of 12 ÷ 0.3. RT wrote, I know 12 ÷ 3 = 4. Since 0.3 is ten times smaller than 3, 12 ÷ 0.3 must be ten times smaller than 4. So 12 ÷ 0.3 = 0.4.

   Did RT get the correct answer? Why or why not?

(Possible answer: RT did not get the right answer. Since 0.3 is ten times smaller than 3, the quotient of $12 \div 0.3$ is ten times larger than the quotient of $12 \div 3$. We can think of division as repeated subtraction. If the size of the piece we are repeatedly subtracting gets ten times smaller, we can repeatedly subtract ten times as many pieces.)

Chapter 4

Measurement and Geometry

The activities in this chapter address common mistakes students make when they solve problems about geometric shapes and solids. When they classify shapes, students sometimes use irrelevant features as defining characteristics of shapes. Students can also develop misconceptions about relationships between classes of shapes when they try to cross-classify shapes (e.g., squares and rectangles). When students measure the volume of three-dimensional shapes, they must think carefully about the relationships between attributes of the shape and common measurement formulas. Students can make mistakes calculating volume if they do not understand how a particular formula connects to the measures of the solid itself. Talking about common geometry mistakes in class can help students develop an explicit awareness of key properties of shapes and solids and form connections between related ideas.

Activity 4.1   Sketching Angles: Thinking Deeply About Right Angles

Activity 4.2   Measuring Area: Clarifying Ideas About Units

Activity 4.3   Classifying Shapes: Comparing Parallelograms and Rectangles

Activity 4.4   Calculating Volume: Counting Hidden Cubes

Activity 4.1   Sketching Angles: Thinking Deeply About Right Angles

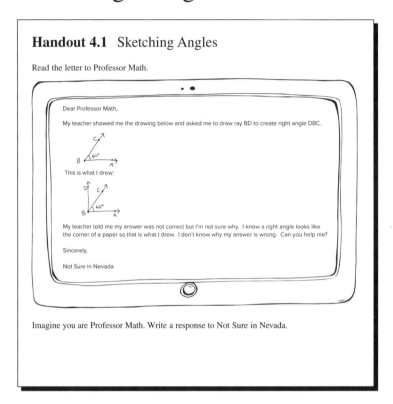

Handout 4.1   Sketching Angles

Read the letter to Professor Math.

Dear Professor Math,

My teacher showed me the drawing below and asked me to draw ray BD to create right angle DBC.

This is what I drew:

My teacher told me my answer was not correct but I'm not sure why. I know a right angle looks like the corner of a paper so that is what I drew. I don't know why my answer is wrong. Can you help me?

Sincerely,

Not Sure in Nevada

Imagine you are Professor Math. Write a response to Not Sure in Nevada.

Overview

In this activity, students examine a mistake related to angle measure. Discussing the error provides students with an opportunity to think about important characteristics of angles and how angles are measured.

Common Core Connections

Measurement and Data, 4.C.5, 4.C.5.A, 4.C.5.B

Before You Use This Activity

Before you use this activity, students should have defined angles as the amount of turning between two rays that share an endpoint. They should know that angles are measured in reference to a 360° circle. They should be familiar with right angles and have had prior experiences using right angles to sketch acute angles, including ones that measure 30°, 45°, and 60°.

Materials (in Appendix)

Handout 4.1, *Sketching Angles*

Digging Deeper into the Math

In grades four and five, students' work in geometry focuses on angles and angle measure. Students learn that the size of an angle is the measure of the amount of rotation, or turning, between the two rays with reference to the 360° circle. Angles can be identified in various ways, including by naming a point on one ray, the common endpoint of the rays (also known as the vertex

of the angle), and a point on the other ray. For example, we can call the 60°
angle in Figure 4.1 angle B, angle CBA, or angle ABC.

Figure 4.1

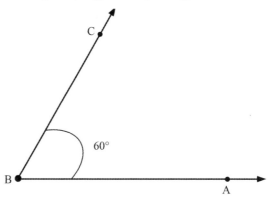

Angles and angle measures are typically difficult concepts for students to
learn. One reason for students' difficulties is their tendency to focus on irrelevant characteristics when they identify, measure, and classify angles. A
common misconception is thinking that the measure of an angle is related to
the length of the rays of the angle rather than the amount of turning between
the rays. For example, many students assert that the two angles in Figure 4.2
have different measures because of the difference in the lengths of the rays.

Figure 4.2

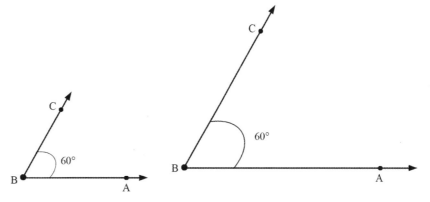

Students may also struggle with angle measure if they have only a narrow
concept of a particular class of angles. For example, if students only see
examples of right angles that look like corners, they may attend to the position of the angle—and not the amount of turning—when they reason about
its measure. (See Figure 4.3.)

Figure 4.3

This misconception may cause students to make errors when they are asked to sketch a right angle with one ray that is not parallel to the horizon. For example, if shown angle CBA (see Figure 4.1) and asked to sketch ray BD to create right angle DBC, some students may focus on creating an angle that looks like a corner. (See Figure 4.4.)

Figure 4.4

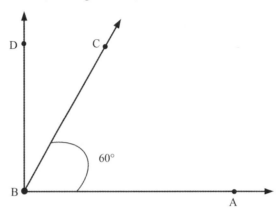

Talking about this error and asking students to sketch right angles that do not look like corners can help students develop understanding of several ideas related to angle measure. First, it can focus students' attention on the importance of turning between two rays as a key characteristic in measuring angles. Second, it can help students understand that the position of an angle on the plane is not related to the measure of that angle. Finally, it can help students measure and create angles by comparing them to benchmark angles, such as 30°, 60°, and 90°.

Teaching Notes

1. Begin by posting the angle featured in this activity (angle ABC) on the board. Ask students to think about where to place ray BD to create angle CBD with a measure of 90°.
2. Pass out Handout 4.1, *Sketching Angles*, and ask students to complete the task. Students should work individually before sharing ideas with a partner. Listen in on students' conversations to help you choose speakers for the upcoming whole-class discussion. (Key ideas to listen for are given in Step 3.)
3. Focus the whole-class discussion on the following key points:
    a. First, talk about why someone might make the mistake featured in the activity. Students may respond that they typically see right angles positioned to look like the corner of a piece of paper.
    b. Second, talk about why the student's answer is wrong. Students should respond that the student has created right angle DBA but was asked to form right angle DBC. If we look at the student's drawing, we can see that angle DBC measures 30°.
    c. Ask for suggestions on how to draw ray BD correctly. Students might suggest drawing another ray straight up from point B to cre-

ate a 30° angle and then doubling the size of this angle to draw ray BD. (See Figure 4.5.)

Figure 4.5

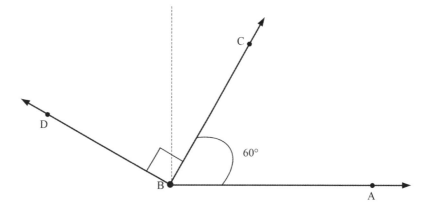

Another strategy is to place the corner of a piece of paper at point B with one edge on ray BC and trace the other edge to draw ray BD.

d. Target the misconception that right angles must look like corners. You might say, "I thought right angles had to look like the corner of a piece of paper. Angle DBC doesn't look like a corner. How can it still be a right angle?" Students should note that the position of the angle does not affect its measure. Angle DBC is a right angle because the amount of turning between rays BD and BC is 90°.

4. Ask students to revise and add on to their original responses to incorporate the ideas from the whole-class discussion.

Extending the Activity

1. Post the drawing (see Figure 4.6) and pose the following prompt to students:

Figure 4.6

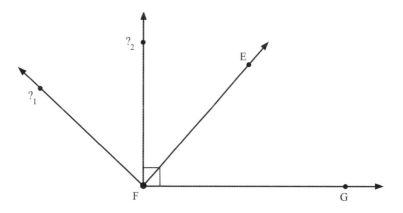

Which question mark should be replaced with the letter H to create angle HFE that measures 90°?

Imagine a friend chose question mark 2 because "right angles should look like corners." What would you say to your friend?

(Possible answer: I would tell my friend that the position of an angle—or the direction it's pointing—does not determine its size. Instead, the size of the opening between the rays that make the angle determines its measure. To find the correct answer, we can use the corner of a piece of paper. If we replace question mark 1 with the letter H to create HFE, a corner of a piece of paper fits perfectly in this angle. This tells us that angle HFE is a right angle.)

2. Post the drawing (see Figure 4.7) and pose the following prompt to students:

Figure 4.7

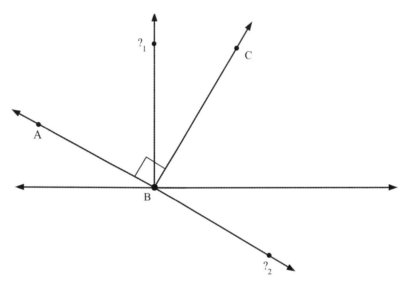

Which question mark should be replaced with the letter D to create a 90° angle with ray BC?

Imagine a friend chose question mark 1 because right angles should go "straight up and down." What would you say to your friend?

(Possible answer: I would tell my friend that right angles do not have to go straight up and down. They can point in any direction. What makes an angle a right angle is the size of the opening between the rays. To find the correct answer, we can use the corner of a piece of paper. If we replace question mark 2 with the letter D, we create the right triangle CBD.)

Activity 4.2   Measuring Area: Clarifying Ideas About Units

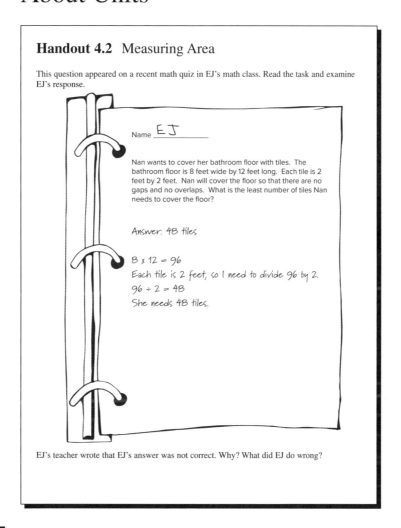

Handout 4.2 Measuring Area

This question appeared on a recent math quiz in EJ's math class. Read the task and examine EJ's response.

Name __EJ__

Nan wants to cover her bathroom floor with tiles. The bathroom floor is 8 feet wide by 12 feet long. Each tile is 2 feet by 2 feet. Nan will cover the floor so that there are no gaps and no overlaps. What is the least number of tiles Nan needs to cover the floor?

Answer: 48 tiles

8 x 12 = 96
Each tile is 2 feet, so I need to divide 96 by 2.
96 ÷ 2 = 48
She needs 48 tiles.

EJ's teacher wrote that EJ's answer was not correct. Why? What did EJ do wrong?

Overview

In this activity, students examine a mistake related to finding the area of a rectangular floor. Discussing the error provides students with an opportunity to connect several important ideas related to two-dimensional measurement.

Common Core Connections

Measurement and Data, 4.A.3

Before You Use This Activity

Before you use this activity, students should understand area as the number of square units it takes to completely cover a shape (without any gaps or overlaps). Students also should have had prior experiences finding the area of a rectangle by multiplying its length and width.

Digging Deeper into the Math

Measuring and solving problems about the areas of rectangles is a major goal of geometry instruction in grades four and five. In prior years, students experience area as the number of square units it takes to completely cover a shape without gaps or overlaps. After initially engaging with this idea using concrete materials, students start to notice the relationship between the arrangement of the tiles and the operation of multiplication. Students eventually move on to using the dimensions of a rectangle to determine its area—without having to show the individual square units inside the shape.

Once students can use the dimensions of a rectangle to calculate its area, they are ready to try more challenging area problems. One particular type of problem focuses on covering an area with a unit larger than the unit square. This task, for example, focuses on the area of a rectangular floor covered by square tiles that measure 2 feet on each side. In the mistake featured in this activity, the student divides the area of the floor by 2 instead of dividing it by 4. Talking about this error provides students with the opportunity to examine and connect several important ideas related to two-dimensional measurement. First, it encourages students to attend to the meaning of the term *square unit* as a square that is one unit by one unit. Second, it helps students think about what happens to the area of a square when its side length is doubled. Finally, it focuses students' attention on the inverse relationship between the size of the unit and the number of units needed to cover an area.

Materials (in Appendix)

Handout 4.2, *Measuring Area*
Graph Paper

Teaching Notes

1. Begin this activity by posting the problem embedded in the task. Ask students to determine the number of 2-by-2-foot tiles needed to cover the 8-by-12-foot floor.
2. Pass out Handout 4.2, *Measuring Area* and copies of graph paper to students. Give students time to think through the task individually before talking with a partner. When students talk with a partner, listen in on their conversations to find speakers for the whole class. (See Step 3 for key ideas to listen for.)
3. Pull the class together for a whole-class discussion.
   a. Begin the discussion by calculating the area of the floor. Be sure students specify the unit of measure for the area of the floor. Students must understand that the term *square feet* refers to squares that are 1 foot long and 1 foot wide (i.e., 1-foot-by-1-foot). When we say that the area of the floor is 96 square feet, we mean that 96 squares—each 1-foot-by-1-foot square—would cover the floor.
   b. Ask why 96 tiles is not the answer to the problem. Students should note that the area of the floor is 96 square feet, which means that 96 1-foot-by-1-foot squares would cover the floor. This is not the answer to the problem, however, because the tiles Nan is using are not 1 foot long.

c. Ask students why someone might make the mistake featured in this activity (i.e., why might someone divide 96 by 2). Students should comment that since each tile is 2 feet long, Nan needs fewer tiles to cover the floor. Since the tiles are twice as long as 1-foot tiles, it may seem reasonable that Nan needs only *half of 96* tiles to cover the floor.

d. Ask students to talk about why the answer is wrong. Students should explain that the tiles are 2-feet-by-2-feet square. That is, they are each 2 feet long and 2 feet wide. This means that the area of each tile is 4 square feet, not 2 square feet.

e. Ask students what the correct answer is. Students should explain that since each tile measures 4 square feet, each tile takes up four times as much area as a 1-foot-by-1-foot square tile. So, the total number of tiles needed is 96 ÷ 4 = 24. Students may benefit from creating a sketch of the problem or using graph paper to draw a model of the floor and the tiles. (See Figures 4.8 and 4.9.)

Figure 4.8 and Figure 4.9

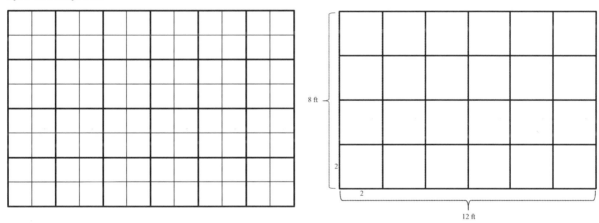

4. Ask students to revise and add on to their original responses to incorporate the ideas from the whole-class discussion.

Extending the Activity

1. Post the task from the main activity. Post the solution shown here and ask students to find and correct the errors.

Solution: 384 tiles
8 × 12 = 96
Each tile is 2 feet by 2 feet or 4 square feet
96 × 4 = 384

(Possible answer: The student found the area of the floor in feet. The floor is 96 square feet. The student made a mistake in the next step when he multiplied 96 × 4. Instead the student should compute 96 ÷ 4. Because the tiles are 2 feet by 2 feet, each tile covers 4 square feet of area. The number of tiles needed to cover the floor is 96 ÷ 4 = 24.)

2. Pose the following prompt to students:

Consider this problem:

BZ wants to tile his 12-feet-by-10-feet kitchen floor with tiles. He will use either 2-feet-by-2-feet square tiles or 3-feet-by-1-foot rectangular tiles. Which choice would require fewer tiles?

Imagine a friend said, "I think the rectangular tiles would require fewer tiles because they are longer than the square tiles." Do you agree or disagree with your friend's answer? Why?

(Possible answer: I disagree with my friend. The area of the rectangular tiles, 3 square feet, is smaller than the area of the square tiles, 4 square feet. This means BZ needs more rectangular tiles to cover the floor than square tiles.)

Activity 4.3   Classifying Shapes: Comparing Parallelograms and Rectangles

Handout 4.3 Classifying Shapes

Read the comic. Then answer the question that follows.

If you were a student in this class, how would you respond to the teacher's questions?

Overview

This activity focuses on the relationship between parallelograms and rectangles. The mistake in the comic strip encourages students to think deeply about how geometric shapes are identified and classified and helps them recognize rectangles as a subset of parallelograms.

Common Core Connections

Geometry, 5.B.3, 5.B.4

Before You Use This Activity

Before you use this activity, students should have prior experiences solving problems about subcategories of geometric shapes. For example, students should understand the relationship between squares and rectangles (i.e., every square is a rectangle) before completing this task.

Materials (in Appendix)

Handout 4.3, *Classifying Shapes*

Digging Deeper into the Math

In grades three through five, a key instructional goal is to identify whether specific examples of geometric shapes are members of certain classes of shapes (e.g., rectangles and parallelograms). To achieve this goal, students must understand that shapes are identified by particular characteristics and that classes of shapes can have hierarchical relationships. For example, rectangles are identified according to their side lengths and angles. Specifically, a shape is a rectangle if it has two pairs of parallel and equal sides and four right angles. Parallelograms are only identified according to their side lengths; they are quadrilaterals with two pairs of parallel sides. Unlike rectangles, angle measure is not a defining characteristic of parallelograms. But because all rectangles satisfy the criteria required for a shape to be a parallelogram, the class of rectangles is a subset of the class of parallelograms. That is, all rectangles are parallelograms. This relationship can be depicted in the Venn diagram in Figure 4.10.

Figure 4.10

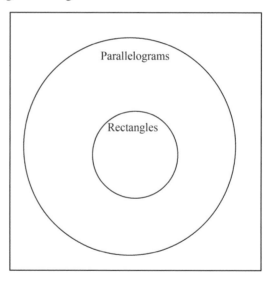

Two misconceptions may prevent students from accepting rectangles as a subset of parallelograms. First, students' experiences with shapes can lead to narrow and inaccurate definitions of shapes. For example, if students have only seen rectangles with two pairs of unequal sides, they may think that all rectangles must have a pair of short sides and a pair of long sides. Second, students' experiences as young learners may lead them to believe that shapes are referred to by one name only. For example, when young students work with pattern blocks, they talk about the orange shape as the orange square but rarely—if ever—refer to it as the orange rectangle! So it is not surprising that older elementary students are confused when we ask them to think about whether one shape can have more than one name or belong to more than one class. Students need to understand that shapes are classified according to particular attributes. Because different classes of shapes may share some of the same key attributes, a shape can be classified or labeled in more than one way if that shape belongs to a subclass of a more inclusive class of shapes. Addressing common misconceptions about shapes is essential for students to develop a robust understanding of how geometric shapes are classified.

1. Begin the activity by posting several examples and nonexamples of rectangles and parallelograms. (See Figures 4.11 and 4.12.) Ask students to draw a few examples of their own. Then ask them to use their drawings to write a definition of each shape.

Figure 4.11

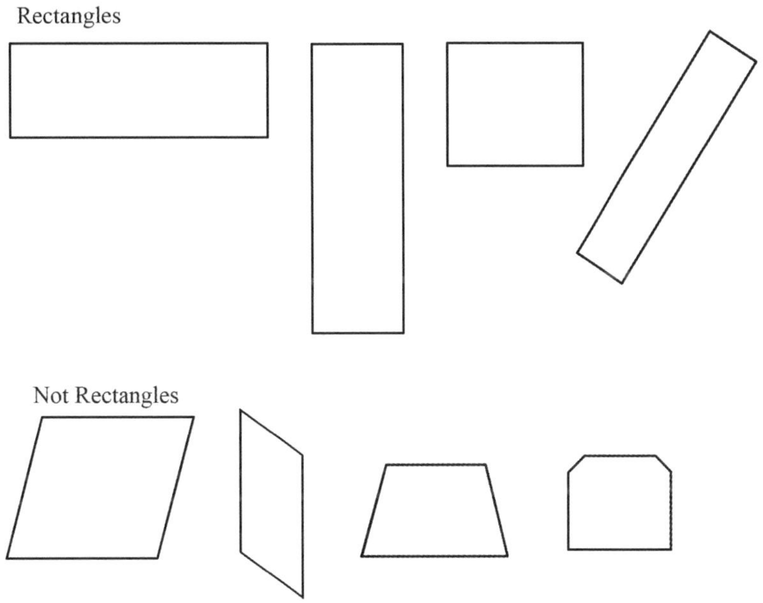

Rectangles

Not Rectangles

Figure 4.12

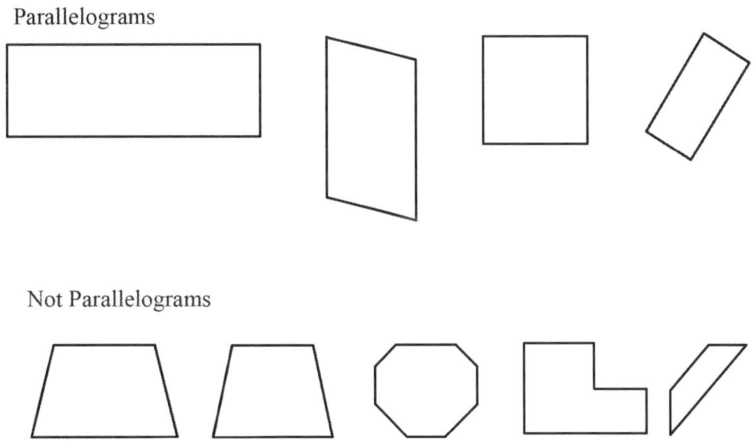

Parallelograms

Not Parallelograms

2. When you conduct the whole-class discussion, keep the talk focused on the following:
   a. Post the following two definitions of rectangle on the board.
      i. A rectangle is a shape with two long sides and two short sides and four right angles
      ii. A rectangle is a shape with two pairs of parallel and equal sides and four right angles
   b. Ask students how the two definitions are similar and different. Then, explain that the most accurate definition for rectangle is the second one. Explain that it is not necessary for one pair of sides to be longer than the other pair for a shape to be classified as a rectangle; that is why we call squares rectangles.
   c. Post the definition for parallelogram on the board: A parallelogram is a quadrilateral with two pairs of parallel sides.
      i. Ask students to determine which shapes (in each of the groups) posted on the board are parallelograms. Students should note that all of the rectangles are parallelograms (in addition to the group of parallelograms). These shapes are parallelograms because they have the characteristics required to be a parallelogram: each is a quadrilateral with two pairs of parallel sides.
      ii. Ask students why we call these shapes *rectangles* and not *parallelograms*. Students should note these shapes are special kinds of parallelograms. They have the characteristics of parallelograms and they also have four right angles.
      iii. Some students may say that parallelograms cannot have right angles. Clarify that this is not true; the size of the angles is not a defining characteristic of parallelograms.
3. Pass out Handout 4.3, *Classifying Shapes*. Give students time to think through the task individually before talking with a partner. When students talk with a partner, listen in on their conversations to find speakers for the whole class. (See Step 4 for key ideas to listen for.)
4. Conduct a whole-class discussion of students' ideas:
   a. Ask students why DD might think the Venn diagram should look like two disconnected circles. Students may respond that DD might think that a shape can only have one label. Or DD might think that parallelograms can't have right angles.
   b. Ask students what the correct Venn diagram should look like. Post the following three possibilities on the board:

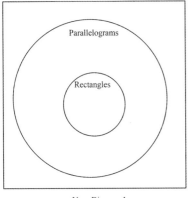

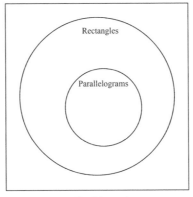

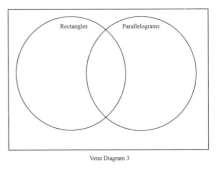

Venn Diagram 1

Venn Diagram 2

Venn Diagram 3

Figures 4.13, 4.14, and 4.15

Students should conclude that the correct choice is choice 1. All rectangles are parallelograms. If a shape is a rectangle, it has two pairs of parallel sides, and so it meets the criteria for a parallelogram. This means that every shape that is a rectangle is also a parallelogram.

   c. Explain to students that we call rectangles a *subclass* of the class of parallelograms.

5. Summarize the activity by explaining that it can be confusing to think of one shape as having more than one label; we typically like to think of things by only one name. But when it comes to geometric shapes, we need to remember that shapes are classified according to certain key attributes. Because different classes share some key attributes, it is possible that a shape can be classified or labeled in more than one way.

Extending the Activity

1. Post the Venn diagram (see Figure 4.16) and pose the following prompt to students:

Figure 4.16

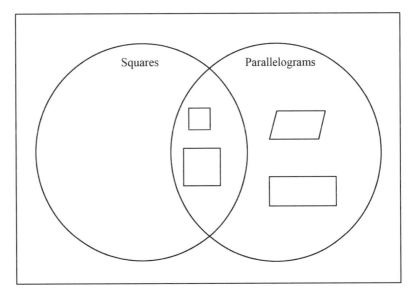

Consider the Venn diagram on the board. Imagine a friend drew this diagram to show the relationship between squares and parallelograms. What do you think about your friend's diagram?

(Possible answer: This is not the most accurate way to represent the relationship. All squares are parallelograms because all squares meet the criteria for a parallelogram—two pairs of parallel sides. It is not possible to make a shape that is a square but not a parallelogram. The diagram would be better if it showed squares as a subset of parallelograms.)

2. Post the Venn diagram and question in Figure 4.17. Then pose the following prompt to students:

Fgure 4.17

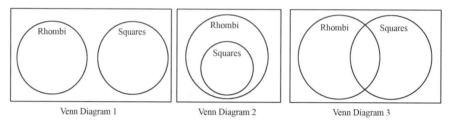

Venn Diagram 1   Venn Diagram 2   Venn Diagram 3

Which of the Venn diagrams is the best choice to show the relationship between rhombi and squares?

Consider the three Venn diagrams and the question on the board. Imagine a friend chose Venn diagram 1 because "squares are straight and rhombi are slanted." What would you say to your friend?

(Possible answer: I would tell my friend that he needs to focus on the most important characteristics of a square and a rhombus. A shape is a square if it has four equal sides and four right angles. A shape is a rhombus if it has four equal sides. This means that every square meets the criteria for a rhombus. The best choice is Venn diagram 2.)

3. Post the Venn diagram in Figure 4.18 and pose the following prompt to students:

Fgure 4.18

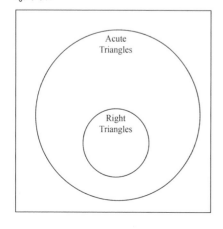

Imagine a friend created this Venn diagram to show the relationship between acute triangles and right triangles because, "All right triangles are also acute triangles because all right triangles have acute angles, too." Do you agree or disagree with the friend's answer?"

(Possible answer: I disagree with my friend's answer. A triangle is classified as a right triangle if it has a right angle. A triangle is classified as an acute triangle if all of its angles are acute, or less than 90°. A triangle is either a right triangle or an acute triangle. It can't be both.)

Activity 4.4   Calculating Volume: Counting Hidden Cubes

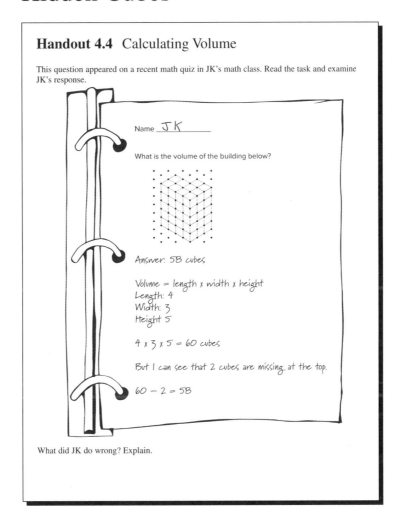

Handout 4.4 Calculating Volume

This question appeared on a recent math quiz in JK's math class. Read the task and examine JK's response.

Name _JK_____

What is the volume of the building below?

Answer: 58 cubes

Volume = length x width x height
Length: 4
Width: 3
Height 5

4 x 3 x 5 = 60 cubes

But I can see that 2 cubes are missing at the top.

60 − 2 = 58

What did JK do wrong? Explain.

Overview

The student work featured in this activity focuses on calculating the volume of an irregular solid. Talking about the mistake featured in the activity provides students with an opportunity to use what they know about the formula $V = l \times w \times h$ to develop strategies for counting *hidden* cubes in irregular geometric solids.

Common Core Connections

Measurement and Data, 5.C.5

Before You Use This Activity

Before you use this activity, students should have had prior experiences finding the volume of right rectangular prisms.

Materials (in Appendix)

Handout 4.4, *Calculating Volume*
Interlocking Cubes (optional)

Students typically use two approaches to find the volume of right rectangular prisms. One approach is to find the product of the length, width, and height. Another is to think about the object in terms of layers—finding the number of cubes or cubic units in one layer and then multiplying this by the total number of layers (i.e., the height of the prism). Students can also adapt these two strategies to find the volumes of irregular solids made up of two rectangular prisms, such as the solid shown in Handout 4.4.

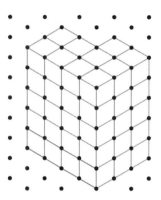

One strategy for calculating the volume of this solid is to imagine it as a $4 \times 3 \times 5$ solid with a piece missing. If students choose this strategy, they may easily derive the expression $4 \times 3 \times 5$ but then struggle to figure out how many cubes are missing. Students may report that there are only two missing cubes because they can only see two cubes missing from the top layer. Talking about this mistake can help students develop a deeper understanding of important ideas related to volume. Discussions about strategies for counting hidden cubes focuses students' attention on volume as a measure of space measured with cubes, not squares. These discussions can also help students make sense of volume in terms of *layers*. Specifically, we can calculate the volume of the missing piece in the figure in Handout 4.4 by reasoning that there are two cubes missing per layer. We can either count the layers by looking at the picture or use the height of the figure, 5, to reason that there are 2×5, or 10, cubes missing. The volume of the figure is $60 - 10 = 50$ cubic units.

1. Begin by posting the problem embedded in the sample student work. Ask students to find the volume of the building using two different strategies.
2. Pass out Handout 4.4, *Calculating Volume*. Ask students to respond to the writing prompt on their own before sharing their ideas with a partner. Use this time to identify speakers for the whole-class discussion. (See Step 3 for suggestions on what to listen for.)

3. Pull the class together for a whole-class discussion.
    a. Generate possible reasons the student, JK, may have written *Volume = length × width × height*. Students will likely recognize this as a formula for calculating the volume of rectangular prisms or boxes.
    b. Talk about how the student, JK, found the length, width, and height. Students may explain that JK probably looked at the base of the solid and counted 4 cubes going back, 3 going across, and 5 squares going up.
    c. Ask students to explain what is wrong with JK's reasoning. Why isn't the product of 4 × 3 × 5 equal to the volume of the building? Students should note that the shape isn't a complete 4 × 3 × 5 rectangular prism because there is a piece missing in the back.
    d. Talk about reasons why JK might have subtracted 2 from 60. Students might note that there are 2 squares, or cubes, missing from the top of the drawing.
    e. Ask students to explain why JK's answer, 58 cubes, is wrong. Students might explain that there are more than just 2 cubes missing from the 4 × 3 × 5 rectangular prism. There are 2 cubes missing from each layer, not 2 cubes missing *in total*.
    f. Talk about how to modify JK's strategy to find the correct volume. For example, we could count that there are 5 layers in the prism. That means that there are 5 × 2, or 10, cubes missing from the complete 4 × 3 × 5 prism. The actual volume is 50 cubic units (60 − 10 = 50).
4. Ask students for other strategies for finding the volume of the solid. For example, students might suggest finding the volume of the 4 × 2 × 5 solid and then adding on the volume of the adjoining 2 × 1 × 5 solid.
5. Wrap up the lesson by asking students to revisit the responses they wrote at the start of the lesson. Students should add on to or revise their answers to incorporate the ideas from the whole-class discussion.

Extending the Activity

1. Show the same irregular solid featured in the main activity, and post the following student response. Ask students to identify and correct the error(s).

    I can see that the top layer has 10 cubes. But I can only see 6 cubes on the layers below this one.
        10 + 6 + 6 + 6 + 6 = 34 cubes

    (Possible answer: The student is correct when she writes that the top layer has 10 cubes. But the student thinks that the other layers only have 6 cubes because she can only see 6 cubes. This is not correct. All the layers are the same; they each have 10 cubes. The volume of the building is 5 × 10 = 50 cubic units.)

2. Show the same drawing featured in the main activity and the following
    student response. Ask students to identify and correct the error(s).

    *I see a 2-by-3-by-5 rectangular prism in the front plus 4 + 2 + 2
    + 2 + 2 cubes behind it. So the volume is 30 + 12 = 42 cubic
    units.*

    (Possible answer: The student is only counting the cubes he can see.
    It would help the student to think of the figure as 2 rectangular prisms.
    One is 2-by-3-by-5 and has 30 cubes. Behind this prism is another
    prism that is 2-by-2-by-5. It has 20 cubes. The total volume of the
    figure is 30 + 20 = 50 cubes.)

Appendix

Decimal Squares

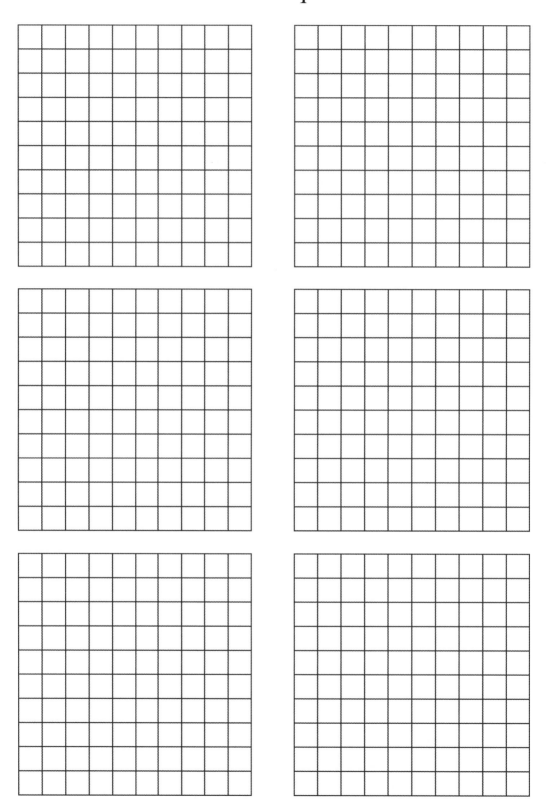

Decimal Number Lines

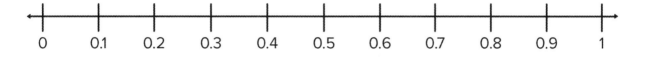

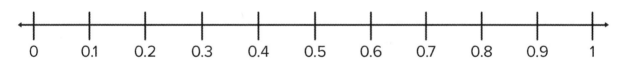

What's Right About Wrong Answers: Learning from Math Mistakes, Grades 4–5 by Nancy C. Anderson. © 2017. Stenhouse Publishers.

Graph Paper

What's Right About Wrong Answers: Learning from Math Mistakes, Grades 4–5 by Nancy C. Anderson. © 2017. Stenhouse Publishers.

Handout 1.1 Comparing Multiplication Models

This task appeared on a recent math quiz in AJ's math class. Read the task and examine AJ's response.

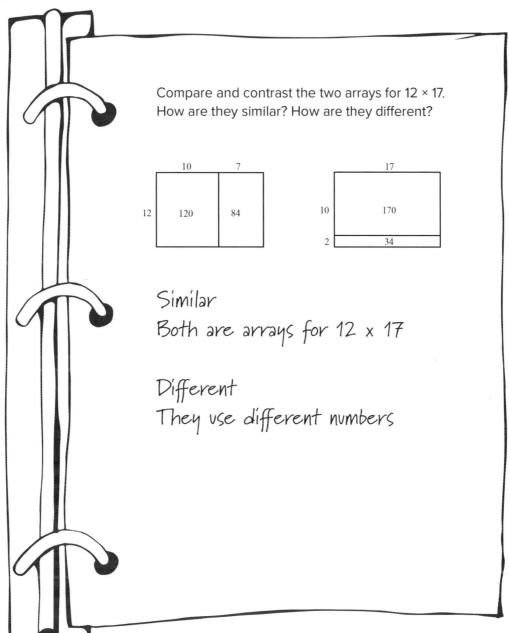

Compare and contrast the two arrays for 12 × 17. How are they similar? How are they different?

Similar
Both are arrays for 12 x 17

Different
They use different numbers

AJ's teacher wrote that AJ's answer was incomplete. Why? What else might AJ have written?

What's Right About Wrong Answers: Learning from Math Mistakes, Grades 4–5 by Nancy C. Anderson. © 2017. Stenhouse Publishers.

Handout 1.2 Solving a Multiplication Word Problem

Read the comic. Then answer the questions that follow.

Questions:
1. Why did BB choose multiplication as a strategy for solving the problem?
2. Is BB's strategy correct? Why or why not?

What's Right About Wrong Answers: Learning from Math Mistakes, Grades 4–5 by Nancy C. Anderson. © 2017. Stenhouse Publishers.

Handout 1.3 Solving a Comparison Word Problem

Read the comic. Then answer the questions that follow.

Questions:
1. Why did JT use the equation 3 × 10 + 10 = 40 to solve the problem?
2. Do you think the price of the sweatshirt is $30 or $40? Explain.

Handout 1.4 Division with Remainders

Read the letter to Professor Math.

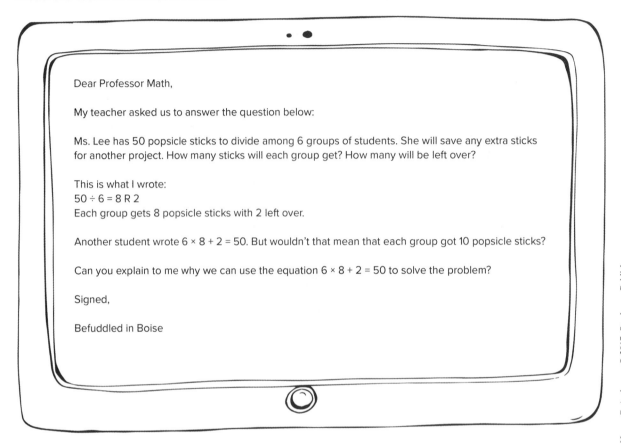

Dear Professor Math,

My teacher asked us to answer the question below:

Ms. Lee has 50 popsicle sticks to divide among 6 groups of students. She will save any extra sticks for another project. How many sticks will each group get? How many will be left over?

This is what I wrote:
50 ÷ 6 = 8 R 2
Each group gets 8 popsicle sticks with 2 left over.

Another student wrote 6 × 8 + 2 = 50. But wouldn't that mean that each group got 10 popsicle sticks?

Can you explain to me why we can use the equation 6 × 8 + 2 = 50 to solve the problem?

Signed,

Befuddled in Boise

Imagine you are Professor Math. Write a response to Befuddled in Boise.

Handout 1.5   Multiplying with Partial Products

A student's work for 23 × 18, 41 × 21, and 36 × 31 is shown. Examine the student's work and then answer the questions that follow.

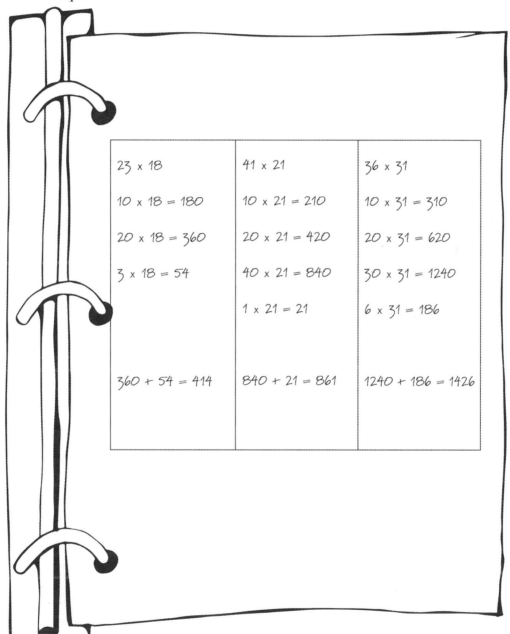

23 x 18	41 x 21	36 x 31
10 x 18 = 180	10 x 21 = 210	10 x 31 = 310
20 x 18 = 360	20 x 21 = 420	20 x 31 = 620
3 x 18 = 54	40 x 21 = 840	30 x 31 = 1240
	1 x 21 = 21	6 x 31 = 186
360 + 54 = 414	840 + 21 = 861	1240 + 186 = 1426

Which computations are correct? Which are incorrect? How might the student correct what's wrong?

What's Right About Wrong Answers: Learning from Math Mistakes, Grades 4–5 by Nancy C. Anderson. © 2017. Stenhouse Publishers.

Handout 1.6 Dividing with Partial Quotients

Read the letter to Professor Math.

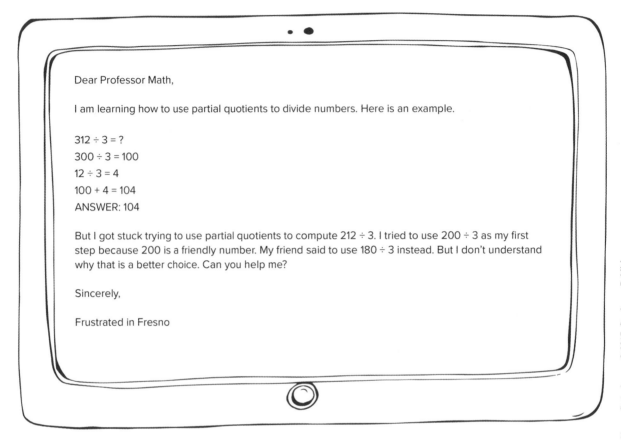

Dear Professor Math,

I am learning how to use partial quotients to divide numbers. Here is an example.

312 ÷ 3 = ?
300 ÷ 3 = 100
12 ÷ 3 = 4
100 + 4 = 104
ANSWER: 104

But I got stuck trying to use partial quotients to compute 212 ÷ 3. I tried to use 200 ÷ 3 as my first step because 200 is a friendly number. My friend said to use 180 ÷ 3 instead. But I don't understand why that is a better choice. Can you help me?

Sincerely,

Frustrated in Fresno

Imagine you are Professor Math. Write a response to Frustrated in Fresno.

What's Right About Wrong Answers: Learning from Math Mistakes, Grades 4–5 by Nancy C. Anderson. © 2017. Stenhouse Publishers.

Handout 1.7 Dividing with Two-Digit Dividends

Read the comic. Then answer the questions that follows.

Questions:
1. Why did DA compute 480 ÷ 10 as the first step in his strategy?
2. Why does DA think it makes sense to compute 48 × 3 as his second step?
3. Does DA's second step, 48 × 3, make sense? Why or why not?

What's Right About Wrong Answers: Learning from Math Mistakes, Grades 4–5 by Nancy C. Anderson. © 2017. Stenhouse Publishers.

Handout 2.1 Working with Unit Fractions

A student, ZZ, solved the following problem. Read the problem and then examine ZZ's work.

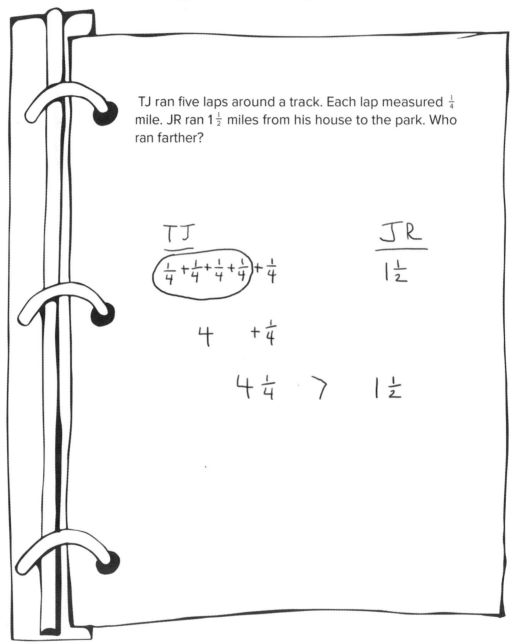

TJ ran five laps around a track. Each lap measured $\frac{1}{4}$ mile. JR ran $1\frac{1}{2}$ miles from his house to the park. Who ran farther?

What mistake did ZZ make? Explain.

What's Right About Wrong Answers: Learning from Math Mistakes, Grades 4–5 by Nancy C. Anderson. © 2017. Stenhouse Publishers.

Handout 2.2 Comparing Fractions

Read the letter to Professor Math.

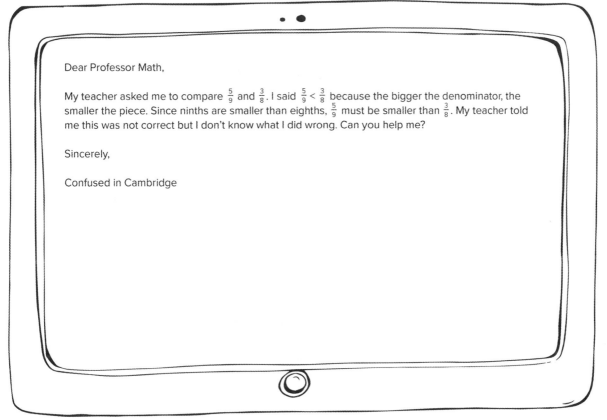

Dear Professor Math,

My teacher asked me to compare $\frac{5}{9}$ and $\frac{3}{8}$. I said $\frac{5}{9} < \frac{3}{8}$ because the bigger the denominator, the smaller the piece. Since ninths are smaller than eighths, $\frac{5}{9}$ must be smaller than $\frac{3}{8}$. My teacher told me this was not correct but I don't know what I did wrong. Can you help me?

Sincerely,

Confused in Cambridge

Imagine you are Professor Math. Write a response to Confused in Cambridge.

What's Right About Wrong Answers: Learning from Math Mistakes, Grades 4–5 by Nancy C. Anderson. © 2017. Stenhouse Publishers.

Handout 2.3 Adding Fractions

Read the comic. Then answer the question that follows.

If you were a student in this class, how would you respond to the teacher's question?

What's Right About Wrong Answers: Learning from Math Mistakes, Grades 4–5 by Nancy C. Anderson. © 2017. Stenhouse Publishers.

Handout 2.4 Subtracting Fractions

Read the letter to Professor Math.

Dear Professor Math:

After I solved the three problems below, my teacher told me to "check my work." The problem is that I don't know what else to do other than look over what I wrote. (And it looks correct to me.) What else can I do to check my work on these problems?

Sincerely,

Baffled in Boston

$$9\frac{3}{4} = 9\frac{6}{8}$$
$$-\ 4\frac{1}{8} = -\ 4\frac{1}{8}$$
$$\boxed{5\frac{5}{8}}$$

$$7\frac{1}{4} = 7\frac{2}{8}$$
$$-\ 3\frac{3}{8} = 3\frac{3}{8}$$
$$\boxed{4\frac{1}{8}}$$

$$8\frac{1}{2} = 8\frac{4}{8}$$
$$-\ 2\frac{7}{8} = 2\frac{7}{8}$$
$$\boxed{6\frac{3}{8}}$$

Imagine you are Professor Math. Write a response to Baffled in Boston.

What's Right About Wrong Answers: Learning from Math Mistakes, Grades 4–5 by Nancy C. Anderson. © 2017. Stenhouse Publishers.

Handout 2.5 Multiplying Fractions

Read the comic. Then answer the question that follows.

Imagine you were a student in LN's class. How would you respond to the teacher's question?

What's Right About Wrong Answers: Learning from Math Mistakes, Grades 4–5 by Nancy C. Anderson. © 2017. Stenhouse Publishers.

Handout 2.6 Dividing Fractions

Two students were asked to compare the expressions $15 \times \frac{2}{3}$ and $8 \div \frac{1}{2}$ using <, >, or =. Examine their work.

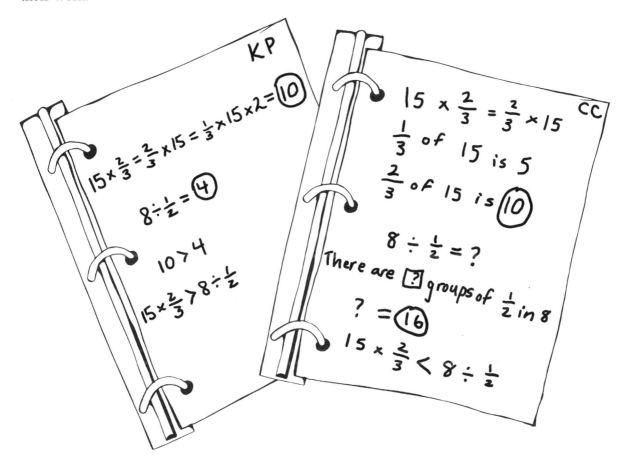

What mistake(s) do you see? Explain.

Handout 3.1 Connecting Fractions and Decimals

Read the letter to Professor Math.

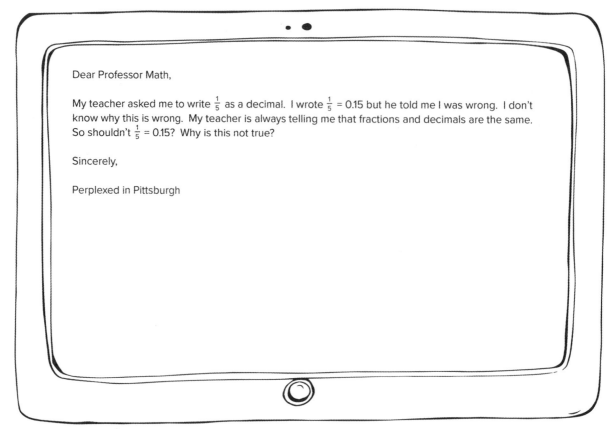

Dear Professor Math,

My teacher asked me to write $\frac{1}{5}$ as a decimal. I wrote $\frac{1}{5}$ = 0.15 but he told me I was wrong. I don't know why this is wrong. My teacher is always telling me that fractions and decimals are the same. So shouldn't $\frac{1}{5}$ = 0.15? Why is this not true?

Sincerely,

Perplexed in Pittsburgh

Imagine you are Professor Math. Write a response to Perplexed in Pittsburgh. Use decimal squares and/or number lines in your response.

What's Right About Wrong Answers: Learning from Math Mistakes, Grades 4–5 by Nancy C. Anderson. © 2017. Stenhouse Publishers.

Handout 3.2 Decimals and Place Value

A student, PH, solved the problem that follows. Read the problem and then examine the student work.

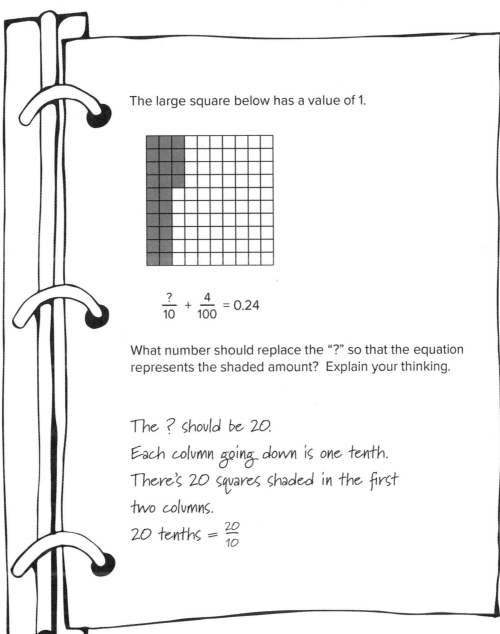

The large square below has a value of 1.

$$\frac{?}{10} + \frac{4}{100} = 0.24$$

What number should replace the "?" so that the equation represents the shaded amount? Explain your thinking.

The ? should be 20.
Each column going down is one tenth.
There's 20 squares shaded in the first
two columns.
20 tenths = $\frac{20}{10}$

What mistake did PH make? Explain.

What's Right About Wrong Answers: Learning from Math Mistakes, Grades 4–5 by Nancy C. Anderson. © 2017. Stenhouse Publishers.

Handout 3.3 Comparing Decimals

Read the letter to Professor Math.

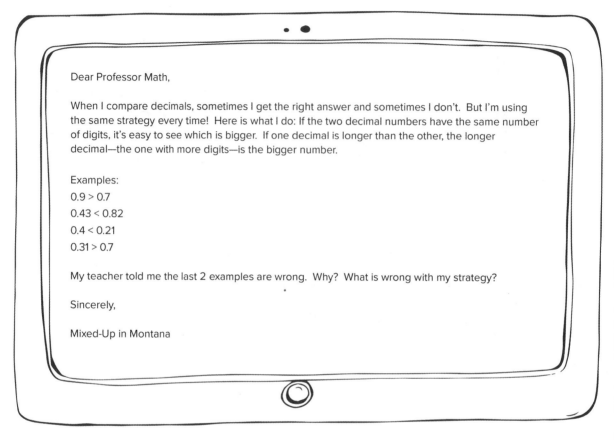

Dear Professor Math,

When I compare decimals, sometimes I get the right answer and sometimes I don't. But I'm using the same strategy every time! Here is what I do: If the two decimal numbers have the same number of digits, it's easy to see which is bigger. If one decimal is longer than the other, the longer decimal—the one with more digits—is the bigger number.

Examples:
0.9 > 0.7
0.43 < 0.82
0.4 < 0.21
0.31 > 0.7

My teacher told me the last 2 examples are wrong. Why? What is wrong with my strategy?

Sincerely,

Mixed-Up in Montana

Imagine you are Professor Math. Write a response to Mixed-Up in Montana. Include decimal squares and/or number lines in your response.

What's Right About Wrong Answers: Learning from Math Mistakes, Grades 4–5 by Nancy C. Anderson. © 2017. Stenhouse Publishers.

Handout 3.4 Subtracting Decimals

A student, EJ, computed 15 – 11.88. His work is shown. Examine EJ's work and then answer the questions that follow.

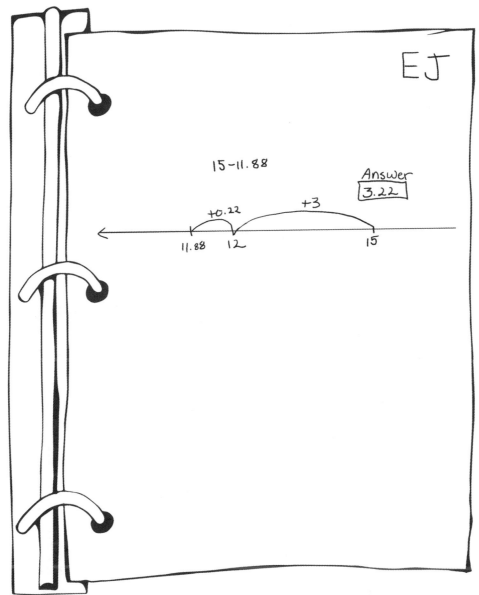

Questions:

1. How is EJ using the number line to compute 15 – 11.88?
2. What did EJ do wrong?
3. How might EJ fix his strategy to find the correct difference?
4. What error might EJ make if he subtracted 12 – 10.77? How might you use a number line to help your friend find and fix his error?

Handout 3.5 Dividing Decimals

Read the comic. Then answer the questions that follow.

Questions:

1. Which strategy do you think gives the correct quotient of 7 ÷ 0.2? Why?
2. What is the other student's mistake?
3. How do you think each student, MJ and LL, might compute 8 ÷ 0.4? Which strategy gives the correct quotient?

What's Right About Wrong Answers: Learning from Math Mistakes, Grades 4–5 by Nancy C. Anderson. © 2017. Stenhouse Publishers.

Handout 4.1 Sketching Angles

Read the letter to Professor Math.

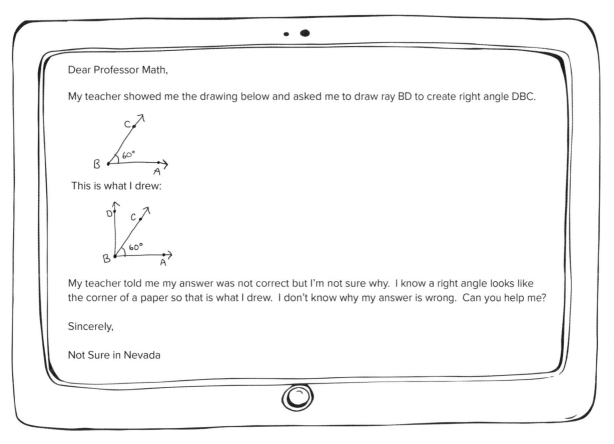

Imagine you are Professor Math. Write a response to Not Sure in Nevada.

Handout 4.2 Measuring Area

This question appeared on a recent math quiz in EJ's math class. Read the task and examine EJ's response.

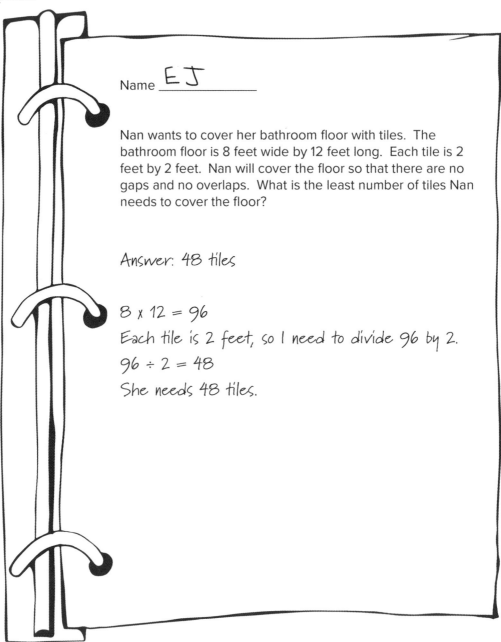

Name **E J**

Nan wants to cover her bathroom floor with tiles. The bathroom floor is 8 feet wide by 12 feet long. Each tile is 2 feet by 2 feet. Nan will cover the floor so that there are no gaps and no overlaps. What is the least number of tiles Nan needs to cover the floor?

Answer: 48 tiles

8 x 12 = 96
Each tile is 2 feet, so I need to divide 96 by 2.
96 ÷ 2 = 48
She needs 48 tiles.

EJ's teacher wrote that EJ's answer was not correct. Why? What did EJ do wrong?

Handout 4.3 Classifying Shapes

Read the comic. Then answer the question that follows.

If you were a student in this class, how would you respond to the teacher's questions?

Handout 4.4 Calculating Volume

This question appeared on a recent math quiz in JK's math class. Read the task and examine JK's response.

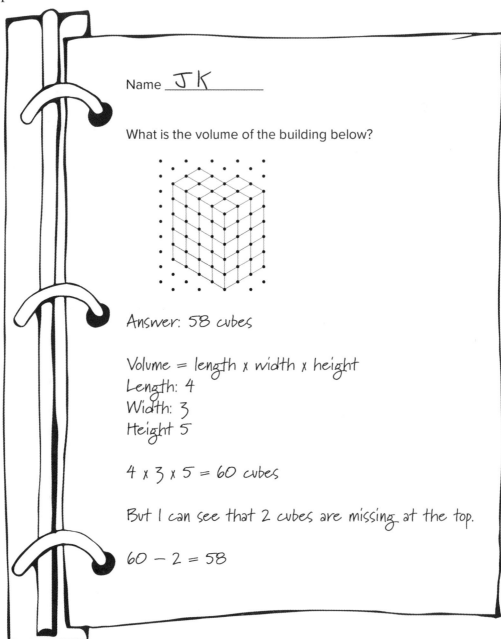

Name __JK__

What is the volume of the building below?

Answer: 58 cubes

Volume = length x width x height
Length: 4
Width: 3
Height 5

4 x 3 x 5 = 60 cubes

But I can see that 2 cubes are missing at the top.

60 − 2 = 58

What did JK do wrong? Explain.

References and Further Reading

Ashlock, Robert. 2010. *Error Patterns in Computation: Using Error Patterns to Help Each Student Learn.* 10th ed. Boston: Allyn and Bacon.

Ball, Deborah, Mark Thames, and Geoffrey Phelps. 2008. "Content Knowledge for Teaching: What Makes It Special?" *Journal of Teacher Education* 59 (5): 389–407.

Bamberger, Honi, Christine Oberdorf, and Karen Schultz-Ferrell. 2010. *Math Misconceptions: From Misunderstanding to Deep Understanding.* Portsmouth, NH: Heinemann.

Boaler, Jo. 2009. *What's Math Got to Do with It? How Parents and Teachers Can Help Children Learn to Love Their Least Favorite Subject.* New York: Penguin.

———. 2016. *Mathematical Mindsets.* San Francisco: Jossey-Bass.

Bransford, John, Ann Brown, and Rodney Cocking. 2000. *How People Learn: Brain, Mind, Experience, and School.* Expanded ed. Washington, DC: National Academy Press.

Brown, Peter, Henry Roediger, and Mark McDaniel. 2014. *Make It Stick: The Science of Successful Learning.* Cambridge, MA: Belknap Press of Harvard University Press.

Collins, Anne, and Linda Dacey. 2010. *Zeroing in on Number and Operations, Grades 5–6.* Portland, ME: Stenhouse.

Dweck, Carol. 2006. *Mindset: The New Psychology of Success.* New York: Ballantine Books.

Franke, Megan, Noreen Webb, Angela Chan, Marsha Ing, Deanne Freund, and Dan Battey. 2009. "Teacher Questioning to Elicit Students' Mathematical Thinking in Elementary School Classrooms." *Journal of Teacher Education* 60: 380–392.

Kazemi, Elham, and Deborah Stipek. 2001. "Promoting Conceptual Thinking in Four Upper-Elementary Mathematics Classrooms." *The Elementary School Journal* 102: 59–80.

McNamara, Julie, and Megan Shaughnessy. 2015. *Beyond Pizzas and Pieces*. 2nd ed. Sausalito, CA: Math Solutions.

Moser, Jason, Hans Schroder, Carrie Heeter, Tim Moran, and Yu-Hao Lee. 2011. "Mind Your Errors: Evidence for a Neural Mechanism Linking Growth Mind-Set to Adaptive Posterror Adjustments." *Psychological Science* 22: 1484–1489.

Rittle-Johnson, Bethany, and Jon Star. 2007. "Does Comparing Solution Methods Facilitate Conceptual and Procedural Knowledge? An Experimental Study on Learning to Solve Equations." *Journal of Educational Psychology* 99 (3): 561–574.

Tirosh, Dina. 2000. "Enhancing Prospective Teachers' Knowledge of Children's Conceptions: The Case of Division of Fractions." *Journal for Research in Mathematics Education* 31: 5–25.

Tobey, Cheryl, and Emily Fagan. 2014. *Uncovering Student Thinking About Mathematics in the Common Core, Grades 3-5*. Thousand Oaks, CA: Corwin.

Tugend, Alina. 2011. *Better by Mistake*. New York: Riverhead Books.

Index